FOREWORD

Canal builders over 200 years ago thought long term, but I doubt whether even they could have envisaged John Rennie's masterpiece being used today, not to carry coal, limestone and slate between Preston, Lancaster and Kendal, but mainly leisure craft, with cyclists, walkers and joggers now enjoying the towpath originally built for working horses. They could certainly not have imagined that 150 years after it was built, their precious asset would be severed in three places at its northern end by a much more destructive mode of successor transport.

The building of the M6 motorway was no doubt the lowest point in the history of the Lancaster Canal, but since then, thanks to the efforts of the Lancaster Canal Trust, the Inland Waterways Association and latterly the Canal and River Trust, we are seeing a renaissance of the waterway that originally connected Kendal to Preston. First, we have seen massive improvements to the navigable part of the canal thanks to the efforts of Mike Macklin's Focus Group involving both the Canal Trust and CRT improvements to moorings, identification of new opportunities for tourism and businesses, and increased volunteer involvement. Second, our CRT operations team under Roy Gibbons is providing a much- improved customer service to all those who use the canal, mainly boaters, but also all the other leisure users. And just as important, we have seen some major infrastructure improvements, to the bridges, to the culverts and most notably, to the Lune Aqueduct.

There is still a long way to go and we still have not managed to fund the restoration of the storm-damaged Stainton aqueduct, but we shall. Now is not a good time to fund major projects. Nevertheless, through the efforts of the Lancaster Canal Regeneration Partnership chaired by Audrey Smith, funding has been secured from South Lakeland District Council, Cumbria County Council and others including IWA and Kendal Town Council to construct a new towpath trail between Kendal and Natland. Jointly, through partnership, we shall continue to achieve improvements, not just on that part of the Lancaster Canal which holds water, but also along the northern corridor where there are so many other opportunities for walkers, cyclists, joggers and those who just want to enjoy the unique landscape.

As we celebrate the Bicentenary of the Lancaster Canal in 2019, we must hold true to the vision of the original canal builders, to complete a waterway link between Preston and the Ribble all the way to Kendal, linking north Lancashire to what is now south Cumbria. It might only be achieved piecemeal in stages, but in the longer term the Northern Reaches ambition will eventually be realised. It must.

Bob Pointing
Chair, North West Partnership, Cana
March 2017

GW00580007

1st edition published in 1989. 2nd ed 2000. 3rd ed 2003. 4th ed 2008. 5th ed 2012

Sixth edition published in 2017. © The Lancaster Canal Trust, 2017

The Lancaster Canal Trust is a Registered Charity No. 1167020
Incorporated Organisation (with limited liability)

Editor for 6th edition: John Laws
Photography: David Currington, Peter Thomas, Graham Agnew, Lynn Agnew,
Richard Trevitt, John Crellin, David Gibson, Phil Metcalfe, David Element and
British Waterways

Milestone Bridge plans reproduced with the permission of Lancashire County
Council and Jacobs UK Ltd.

Designed by Graham Agnew, info@thedrawingroom-design.co.uk
Printed by Kent Valley Printers, Kendal

Maps are drawn to a scale of 1:25,000, contains OS data © Crown copyright and
database right 2017

ISBN 978-0-9514146-5-1

CONTENTS

EDITOR'S NOTE for the 6th EDITION

It is hard to believe that the 5th Edition of the Guide book is now five years old and requiring an updated replacement to take account of all sorts of changes that have occurred, particularly with the business enterprises featured on the map pages. Some have succumbed to the tough economic times and closed down, some have changed their name or other details and indeed some new ones have been born. The narrative sections have also been reviewed, amended and brought up to date. We hope we have succeeded in keeping abreast of these changes.

Also during the life of the 5th Edition the transfer of the inland waterways into the charity sector with the establishment of the Canal & River Trust (C&RT) and the demise of British Waterways has been completed.

There were numerous references to BW in previous editions. Where these related to the history of the canal, or to past events, the name BW lives on in these pages. In the context of current and future activities the title Canal & River Trust has been adopted.

Every effort has been made to ensure the accuracy of the information in this book. Please let us know if you find any errors or changes. Lancaster Canal Trust cannot accept any liability for loss, injury or damage resulting from the use of the information in this book.

As always, the work of contributors of both text and photographs in earlier editions is acknowledged, as is the assistance of numerous colleagues in the task of identifying necessary changes and in the preparation of the new book.

John Laws
Lancaster, March 2017

The Canal & River Trust

Canal &
River Trust

Responsibility for inland waterways belongs to the **Canal & River Trust**

ABOUT THIS BOOK

This is a book for dipping into rather than reading from cover to cover! Whatever it is that brings you to the canal we hope you find something of interest in one or more sections of the book. Browse in the winter evenings while planning your next cruise; carry it with you on foot or on a boat. We make no apology for any repetition of information between the various sections and we hope we have justified the use of the word 'Complete' in the title!

The guide covers the Lancaster Canal from Preston to Kendal, including the Ribble Link and the branch to Glasson Dock and the narrative is written as if making a journey from south to north. Follow the accompanying maps from the bottom of each page and work up. For the journey from north to south a little more patience is required to follow the text in reverse!

However, to help you determine your location as you travel, all the bridges are identified with a number plate on each side, as far north as Bridge 172 at Stainton. The bridge numbers are on these maps.

The mileposts found along the canal are also marked on these maps, with a symbol showing mileage *to* Kendal and *from* Preston. On the canal south of Lancaster they are cast iron plates mounted on stone posts and give mileages between Preston and Garstang and between Garstang and Lancaster. North of Lancaster they are engraved stone posts and give mileages between Lancaster and Kendal. Several are missing and it is planned to replace them and restore damaged ones in time for the canal's bicentenary in 2019.

Ordnance Survey coordinates are given for some facilities which are not immediately adjacent to the canal.

GEOGRAPHY OF THE LANCASTER CANAL

Lancashire and Cumbria are counties of contrast. To the south, in Lancashire, lie the great conurbations of Manchester and Liverpool, whilst in the north are the Lake District and the Howgills. To the east, the Pennines form a natural boundary. South of the River Lune the rolling heather clad hills of the Forest of Bowland offer easy walking with fine views across the Fylde plain to the sea. In the valleys of the Lune, Wyre and Ribble there are picturesque villages and winding lanes. To the east of Carnforth, North Yorkshire juts into Lancashire to within 10 miles of the coast. To the west is Morecambe Bay and the Irish Sea, and the coastal resorts of Lytham St. Annes, Blackpool, Fleetwood and Morecambe.

The Area of Outstanding Natural Beauty around Arnside and Silverdale offers some of the finest countryside anywhere, yet is missed by many a motorist driving up the M6, eager to get to the Lakes or Scotland.

Both counties are rich in history. Vikings, Romans, have all left their mark on the landscape. The castles at Lancaster, Clitheroe and Kendal bear witness to the more troubled times of the past. But perhaps the most important time in Lancashire's history was the Industrial Revolution. The canal age began with the Bridgewater Canal just outside Manchester whilst the sons of Lancashire pioneered many inventions that were to make the county one of the most important industrial areas in the country, founded on cotton. Unfortunately, cotton is no longer king, but the decline of the industry has enabled the county to cast off its image of 'dark satanic mills', although its past importance is remembered in several museums devoted to this aspect of Lancashire life. Cumbria never achieved the industrial status of its southern cousin, but utilised its natural assets – gunpowder manufacture being an important industry in the villages south of Kendal, whilst the quarrying of limestone and slate is still an important feature of the local economy.

Lancaster's importance goes back to Roman times when it was a fortified crossing point on the River Lune on the main route to Scotland. It developed further in the eighteenth century as the main port on the west coast prior to the development of Liverpool, leaving a legacy of many fine buildings and past industries based on Lancaster's important trade with the African colonies and the New World. Robert Gillow, the furniture manufacturer famous the world over, founded his business in Lancaster using the tropical hardwoods that were being imported through the port.

Through it all runs the Lancaster Canal, built to transport coal north and limestone south, almost bisecting the area and making it an ideal base for those wishing to explore the riches of this part of the world. Whether you come for a day, a week or a month, North Lancashire and South Cumbria have so much to offer. It is not possible to include in this guide everything there is to see and do along the canal, but it is intended to provide a flavour of what is there, so that the visitor can plan a rewarding visit, whatever its length.

HISTORY OF THE LANCASTER CANAL

In the middle of the Eighteenth Century, Lancaster was a prosperous town and port. Ideally situated on the west coast, it was the main route between the old and the new worlds. Manufactured goods from the industries of Lancashire and Yorkshire left the country through Lancaster for the developing Americas. Ships returning from this rich new territory brought in produce which formed the basis for much of Lancaster's industry and prosperity, whilst a few miles to the north at Kendal, snuff and tobacco curing established itself. But there were ominous signs on the horizon! As ships grew in size, so did the difficulties of navigating the notorious estuary of the River Lune, thus threatening the prosperity of Lancaster (and the smaller port of Milnthorpe), whilst to the south Liverpool was growing in importance.

In an effort to save Lancaster, the merchants proposed building a canal starting at Kendal and running almost due south through Lancaster to Preston, from where it would run south-westwards, passing through Leyland and the village of Parbold to join the Leeds & Liverpool Canal, thus providing a direct link between Lancaster and the port of Liverpool. The famous canal engineer James Brindley, responsible for the construction of much of England's early canal network, was asked to make a survey, though it is more likely that his pupil Robert Whitworth undertook the work.

The scheme did not attract much support in the town. An alternative idea of building a new port at Glasson at the mouth of the Lune found favour and the idea of a canal was dropped. However, there was still a group who extolled the virtues of having Lancaster on the canal map and in the 1790's John Rennie was asked to re-survey the canal. Rennie's proposal followed much of Whitworth's original route to Preston, but here Rennie's line crossed the Ribble then struck out south-eastwards towards Chorley, thence east of Wigan to Westhoughton, for Rennie was basing his canal, not on trade with America, but on coal from the South Lancashire coalfield and limestone from quarries around Kendal and Milnthorpe. Rennie knew from what had happened on the Bridgewater Canal just how valuable a cargo of coal could be, fuelling industry and home alike, but how difficult its carriage on land could be. Limestone was important not only for building purposes, but also as a soil conditioner and would be in demand in the agricultural belt of West Lancashire. The fact that Rennie proposed that the canal should be capable of taking broad beam craft, up to seventy two feet in length, is an indication that he had designs on linking the canal to the Bridgewater Canal, and thus the main canal system. In the event this did not happen.

Rennie's proposals found favour throughout Lancashire and south Westmorland (as this part of Cumbria was then known). An Act of Parliament was obtained and construction began in 1792. The company was dogged by financial problems from the start and by the end of the century only the section from Wigan to Walton Summit, five miles south of Preston, and the section northwards from Preston to Tewitfield had been completed, the two sections being linked by a temporary tramway. Eventually, in 1819 the canal was opened through to Kendal and by 1826 a branch to Glasson Dock had been built. The northern and southern sections were never linked by water, the tramway becoming permanent. The southern section became part of the Leeds & Liverpool canal from Johnson's Hillock to Wigan, having been first leased, and then sold, to the Leeds and Liverpool Canal Company. Despite not being linked to the main network, the canal flourished, carrying not only coal and limestone, but all manner of goods, until the coming of the railways.

At first the railways did not pose a threat, for by the mid Nineteenth Century the spread of metals from the Midlands had only reached Preston. The canal company had introduced passenger carrying boats and these provided the most comfortable means of transport then available for travellers in North Lancashire, the 'packet' boats completing the trip from Kendal to Preston (and vice versa) in around eight hours. Even the building of the Lancaster and Preston Railway did not pose a threat; upon its opening the canal company immediately halved its tolls on goods carried on the canal and withdrew the packet boat service south of Lancaster. The effect was to force the railway to rely on a small amount of passenger traffic, something it could not afford to do; this set the scene for something almost unique in waterways history, that of a canal company taking over a railway, and for a time the railway and canal operated alongside one another.

The proposal to build a railway between Carlisle and Lancaster was another matter, since this would take the tracks not only into the area served by the canal, but beyond! The proposal was vigorously opposed by the canal company, but to no avail. Matters were further complicated because the act authorising the railway's construction conferred powers to link into the track of the Lancaster and Preston Railway and also to run through trains to Preston and the South. The canal company tried to fight back by providing as much hindrance as possible to through traffic on the railway, but the final nail in the coffin came when an accident occurred at Bay Horse, south of Lancaster. An express from Carlisle ran into the rear of a local train from Lancaster, with a resultant loss of life. After this the canal company was instructed not to resist the passage of trains from the Lancaster & Carlisle Railway and the canal became unable to compete. Eventually, the canal was leased by the then London & North Western Railway Company and later bought outright, a special medal being struck to commemorate the event. In 1885 the Lancaster Canal Company ceased to exist and this chapter in the history of the canal closed.

Despite this, the railway continued to operate the canal, finding it to be an excellent supply of water for depots at Preston, Lancaster and Carnforth, but now the railways were facing competition – this time from the roads. Canal traffic through to Kendal ceased in 1944 and

the final commercial load carried on the canal was a consignment of coal from Barrow, via Glasson Dock to Storey's at Lancaster in 1947. From Kendal to Stainton the canal was progressively dewatered, having suffered great losses of water through seepage into the porous limestone over which the canal is built. In the 1960's, the Ministry of Transport proposed culverting the canal north of Carnforth in six places, thus denying access to this lovely section of canal. Despite vigorous opposition the Ministry's plans went ahead as the M6 motorway was extended northwards, leaving only forty two of the original fifty seven miles of canal north of Preston open to traffic.

Following the transfer of ownership to the London & North Western Railway Company, the grouping of railways in 1923 led to a further transfer to the London, Midland & Scottish Railway. With railway nationalisation in 1948, control passed to the British Transport Commission, and subsequently by the 1962 Transport Act to the British Waterways Board. The latest in this series of major changes is the transfer to the charity sector in 2012 with the establishment of the Canal & River Trust.

What remains of the tramway is in the control of Preston City Council and is a public right of way, providing an interesting route for a walk or cycle ride, south from Avenham Park in Preston to Bamber Bridge. Further south, the site of the transfer basin from the tramway to the Southern Section of the Lancaster Canal is now lost in a housing estate at Clayton Brook, but the line of the canal can be found at Whittle-le-Woods (bridge and tunnel) before the remaindered arm of the canal can be seen at its junction with the Leeds & Liverpool Canal at Johnson's Hillock.

COKE OVENS ON THE LANCASTER CANAL

There are several banks of coke, or cinder, ovens along the northern section of the Lancaster Canal. These were used to make coal into coke. They are all located at the canal side opposite the tow path, with a wharf access for unloading of the coal from the canal after transport from the Lancashire coalfields, and road access to export the coke for local use. They are located near villages with a demand for the product and are often associated with a coal wharf. They probably developed later to supplement the coal sales. After closing they were often used by locals as recreation attractions.

Coke was used as a smokeless fuel for domestic use and for small industrial use e.g. by blacksmiths and bakers. As well as its reduced smoke and fume properties it has a much more consistent and long lasting burn than coal. Other uses may have been for static steam engines or road traction engines. On an industrial scale it was used in iron smelting because it burned at a higher temperature than coal. Coke is a purified form of carbon without the tar impurities in coal which could contaminate products.

The Lancaster Canal coke ovens are of a village scale since they were for local use. They occur in sets of 4 to 6 which suggests a rotating batch process with one being fired with others being filled and emptied. The process is similar to that of charcoal production but coal, rather than wood, is baked. The oven is kept burning at a low rate using only the gases given off as fuel. Air, or oxygen, is limited as much as possible. They are called 'beehive' ovens because of the similarity of their domed shape and are often buried in a bank.

The ovens were developed as the coal traffic developed but seem to have declined fairly soon with competition from commercial gas works which produced coke as a by-product.

Gazetteer From north to south, locations of each are marked on the canal maps. The Holme ovens have an information board on a plinth on the towpath opposite the ovens.

Kendal   SD 520918
No trace. Now a sports field.

Crooklands   SD 534836
No trace. Now a Coal Yard.

Holme   SD 528786
Visible. On private land.

Tewitfield   SD 528785
In a private back garden.

Carnforth   SD 494695
The wharf and back wall of the ovens are visible from the canal and the front is accessible along the footpath over the nearby bridge.

Bolton-le-Sands SD 488688
Covered in spoil. Being uncovered.

Lancaster   SD 488636
By aqueduct. Visible

Ellel   SD 483541
In quarry and visible.

ENGINEERING OF THE CANAL

Several of the prominent canal engineers of the 18th and 19th centuries had a hand in building the Lancaster Canal. The initial surveys were commenced in 1771 by James Brindley and completed in 1772 by Robert Whitworth but it is John Rennie whose name is most firmly linked with the Lancaster Canal. In the five years between 1792 and 1797 he steered the project from its enabling Act of Parliament to the completion of the majority of its length. He refined and modified the earlier surveys, taking the canal along the western edge of the Pennine hills at 72 feet above sea level for 43 miles from Preston to Tewitfield.

The final route of the canal took a north-south line with remarkably little deviation; the one large detour west in to the Fylde had little to do with topography but was influenced by an original plan to build a canal branch to Fleetwood. Where the hills meet the coastal plain three different centuries of transport development and four major systems – the canal, the railway, the A6 and the M6 – are seldom far apart and in several places are all within the space of a quarter of a mile. The modern energy transmission systems, overhead cables and underground pipelines, also share the same corridor.

Twenty-two years passed before the canal reached Kendal. Between 1813 and 1819 the 14 mile northern section was built, along with a flight of eight broad locks at Tewitfield which raised the canal to the 146 foot level. The Engineer was William Crosley Jnr, whose father, also William, had been an assistant both to Rennie and to another prominent canal engineer, William Jessop. The Glasson branch was opened in 1826, connecting the canal to the sea at Glasson Dock. It is 2½ miles long with 6 locks and was also engineered by Crosley Jnr, who then went on to become Engineer on the Macclesfield Canal.

The early canals tended to follow the lie of the land at a certain contour level – hence the term 'contour canal' – and were often somewhat circuitous as a result. The necessary civil engineering skills to straighten the line with deep cuttings and large embankments had not yet been perfected. However, on the Lancaster Canal there are substantial cuttings at Salwick (Br.25–27) and Ashton Road (92–94), and major embankments at Burton-in-Kendal and Sedgwick, where three aqueducts (144, 145 & 178) carry the canal over minor roads. The canal is also carried high over the traffic at Bulk Road / Caton Road (Br.106 rebuilt and widened in 1961) and in Preston, where, although the structure was demolished in 1964, the name lives on in Aqueduct Street.

The one tunnel on this canal is at Hincaster, 378 yards long, with the portals and invert in ashlar limestone masonry and the rest lined in brick. Brick is an unusual material on the Lancaster Canal, as the canal's trustees were unused to it and insisted that Rennie mostly used masonry, with which they were more familiar. In fact, brickmaking skills were not to be found locally and men were brought from the midlands to make the bricks nearby at Heversham. The tunnel portals are listed structures and the adjacent Horsepath, leading a half a mile over the hill, is a Scheduled Ancient Monument.

Rennie designed and built 22 aqueducts and more than 80 culverts to carry the Lancaster Canal over the many rivers in this area which flow predominantly from east to west across the line of the canal. Some are tiny but graceful masonry culverts for minor streams, some are substantial structures. Those over Barton Brook (Br.38) and the Rivers Brock (46), Wyre (61), Conder (87), and Keer (132) are especially notable. Many of them are accessible by steps from the towpath. Where the river level was too close to the canal level a weir was constructed and the river level lowered to give clearance beneath the structure; in two cases a siphon dives under the canal, discharging the river back at its original level (Br.52 and between 91 & 92).

The most imposing structure is of course the massive Lune aqueduct, described as "...without doubt the finest and largest example of a masonry aqueduct in the country" by L.T.C.Rolt in 'Navigable Waterways'. It is widely regarded as one of the wonders of the English canal system. Its five semicircular arches carry the canal 51 feet above the river. The resident engineer for the foundations in the river, William Cartwright, received a special presentation from the Company for his work.

In 2011 the Grade 1 listed aqueduct underwent an extensive programme of restoration and enhancement, funded by British Waterways and the Heritage Lottery Fund. The channel was drained and the masonry pointed and grouted. The exterior was inspected and pointed by roped access. Intrusive vegetation was removed from the structure, graffiti cleaned off and damaged balustrades repaired. Access between the towpath and the riverside path below was improved with widened steps and new paths. During these works it was possible to see and appreciate at close range the enduring quality of the 18th century masonry. On the middle span there are friezes above the arch with inscriptions. The upstream face reads: 'To Public Prosperity' whilst the downstream side bears a Latin inscription that translates as: 'Old needs are served, far distant sites combined. Rivers by art to bring new wealth are joined.'

Having built the Lune aqueduct, the Canal Company had insufficient funds for the comparable crossing of the River Ribble. In Lancaster Maritime Museum's splendid section devoted to the canal there are two drawings for the proposed Ribble aqueduct signed by both John Rennie and William Jessop and dated May 12th 1801. They show a graceful masonry structure with three elliptical arches each spanning 116 feet. This would have been the second largest structure on the canal and its absence had a major influence on the development of the canal. The 'temporary' tramway which took its place was first proposed by Cartwright and developed by Benjamin Outram. It connected the two separate parts of the canal for more than 50 years; it is described in the History section.

There are many interesting engineering features relating to the original route between Preston and Westhoughton but as this is no longer part of the Lancaster Canal they are outside the scope of this book.

Nearly 200 bridges span the canal, with a clear passage of 14 feet for barges and a towpath for the horses. Almost all the original bridges are masonry arches, with the stone quarried locally near the canal; some of the loading wharves on the canalside can still be seen. Most were designed by Rennie and well over half of them are now listed structures. There are several 'standard patterns', with differences in the detailing of parapets and abutments, perhaps according to the contractor of the various sections of the canal. Three changeline bridges (98, 100 & 186) cleverly take the towpath both under and over the bridge to the opposite side of the cut. A number of bridges with a significant skew angle demonstrate the finer points of the masons' craft in the complex geometry of the stone blocks. It is a tribute to Rennie and to the inherent strength of the arch design that huge articulated trucks now pass over many of the bridges, although limitations of road alignment and clearance have lead to an increasing number of 'bridge strikes', with damage to parapets and concern for the safety of those below on the water or on the towpath. Many bridges have been widened over the years, with varying degrees of sensitivity: some almost seamlessly in masonry, some gracefully with cambered cast iron beams, some with riveted wrought iron girders, some quite brutally in utilitarian steel or concrete.

Water supply and control has always been fundamental to the success of any canal and the Lancaster is no exception. An Act of Parliament of 1819 enabled the construction of Killington Reservoir, 5 miles east of Kendal. This feeds water via Peasey Beck to Crooklands, where a weir and 1/2 mile channel divert it into the canal. Stainton Beck also supplies the canal and these two feeders account for the fact that the canal is still in water this far north; they are the principal sources for the entire canal, providing water for the locks on the branches and making up for evaporation, leakage and seepage. Several other rivers and becks and numerous field drains deliver water at various points along the whole length of the canal. It is ironic that the motorway, which so devastated the northern reaches, actually helps keep the canal topped up by discharging its storm water drainage, through oil interceptors, into the canal. At various places overflow weirs can be seen, mostly on the offside, where excess water is discharged into a stream passing below the canal. Many of the bridge passages are equipped with grooves on either side where stop planks can by inserted to dam the water in the event of a breach or to enable

a section to be drained for maintenance. The northern reaches suffered greatly from leakage into the porous limestone rock and two bridges in this area were fitted with mitre gates for water control; Br.146 had one pair facing north and Br.170 had two pairs, covering both directions. The gates are long gone but the recesses in the bridge passage can still be seen.

In 2002 the Lancaster Canal finally gained a connection with the rest of the inland waterway network with the opening of the Millennium Ribble Link. This made use of the unlikely looking, narrow and winding, Savick Brook. Its level is now controlled by a rising sector gate near the tidal Ribble estuary and by five locks along a two mile length, with a three rise staircase lock making the connection into the main line of the canal near bridge 16. The Link itself and the transit to the Leeds & Liverpool Canal at Tarleton are described elsewhere in this book.

Construction of the M6 north of Carnforth in the 1960s, together with the lack of boat traffic and high maintenance costs, resulted in the canal being closed to navigation north of Tewitfield, a section now known as the Northern Reaches. South of Crooklands (Br165) the canal was retained to link the feeder from Killington Reservoir via Peasey Beck to the navigable canal, albeit at a low, unnavigable level with weirs.

From Crooklands to Stainton (Br172) the canal is designated a 'remainder' canal. It is navigable but disconnected, it is used to connect to a secondary feeder at Stainton. The Lancaster Canal Trust's trip boat *Waterwitch* is the only permanently powered craft on this stretch.

The plans for restoration of the Northern Reaches are described later in this book under the heading 'The Future for the Lancaster Canal'.

Milestone Bridge

The new bridge over the Canal carries the M6 link road the 'Bay Gateway', it is between Br 111 & 112 to the north of Lancaster between Beaumont and Torrisholme. 'Milestone Bridge' is close to to the milestone Lancaster 3, Kendal 24 miles. The bridge is precast and consists of 30 pairs of arch beams installed in December 2014 using a pair of 200 tonne mobile cranes. Its single span of 28.7m is claimed to be the longest spanning twin precast arch beam bridge in the UK. The design of the arch profile allows for a canal width of 11.3m and head room of 3.5m with a min 2.0m wide x 2.30m high envelope on the towpath side and 4.50m wide x 4.25m high envelope on the off side

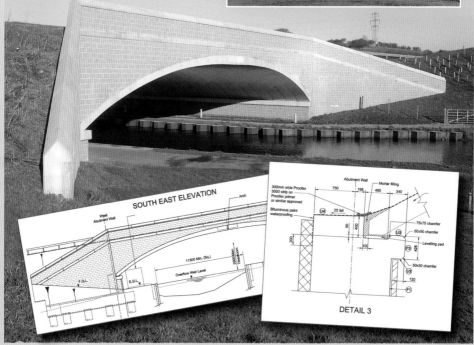

SOUTH EAST ELEVATION

DETAIL 3

ECOLOGY OF THE LANCASTER CANAL

The canal forms a valuable wildlife corridor through towns and farmland. Originally man made, it has become naturalised over time, enabling species to survive and thrive where otherwise they would be unable. A walk along the towpath is, effectively, a walk into the heart of the countryside, even though you may only be a stone's throw from human habitation, a built-up environment or an area of intensive agriculture.

The whole of the Lancashire section of the canal is designated a Biological Heritage Site and is the largest and most species-rich water body in the county. It supports a wide variety of plants and animals that are typical of slow flowing water bodies. Around 250 plants have been recorded along the length of the canal, including a number of rarities such as the great spearwort, the three-leaved water crowfoot, white water lily and the horned pondweed. There is also a rare hybrid horsetail that occurs in only one locality in Lancashire, close to the Cumbrian border.

The canal is at its best in summer, when the banks are rich in wild flowers, but each season has its own charms, as seed heads and berries grace the autumn days and winter frost can be spectacular on the skeletons of waterside plants. In spring everything becomes new again and trees are bursting with buds whilst birds are busy breeding and nesting.

Along the canal several different plant habitats run in parallel; the true aquatic plants, the marginals (which have their roots in the water but otherwise grow above it), the water-loving meadow plants, the hedgerows, which line the towpath, and finally the trees. Watch how the plant communities change as you walk or ride along, sometimes through wooded cuttings, sometimes in the open. Also notice how the underlying condition of the banks affect the ecology. The old collapsed banks have the richest variety of species. The disturbed ground of restored or newly cut banks, or the upgraded towpaths, are generally more sparsely vegetated by a limited variety of colonising species, but other species soon follow.

In the open reaches the fluffy-headed meadow sweet is relatively common, often occurring with yellow-flag iris. There are drifts of reedmace (bulrush), conspicuous with its characteristic brown pokers, and Rosebay willow herb, which is especially striking in the late summer. There is water mint, wild angelica, marjoram, various vetches, buttercups, and many more. At the northern end of the canal a change in plant species reflects the change in the underlying rock to limestone. Here you will find harebells, lady's bedstraw, cut-leaved cranesbill, and other calcium loving plants.

Along the hedges are blackberries, elder, hawthorn and blackthorn. In the wooded cuttings, shelter from wind and the low levels of light produce a different association of plants. In spring the unmistakable smell of wild garlic fills the air. In autumn, hart's tongue and other ferns become more notable and the ready supply of rotting wood supports a rich variety of fungi. The cutting at Salwick is a good example of mixed woodland where trees such as beech colour up particularly well in the autumn. Elsewhere, trees have been planted or have colonised naturally along the waters edge. Ash is relatively common. Larch was planted both as a windbreak on exposed sections and as a resource to provide timber for canal maintenance work.

The stone walls provide a discrete environment for ferns, mosses and lichens. Most people are familiar with the floating round leaves and flowers of the water lily in summer, but the plants can also be seen in winter, if the water is clear, growing like cabbages on the canal bottom.

Bird life is abundant. On the water, look out for mallards, coots, moorhens and mute swans. These are especially prevalent in the built-up areas, tempted by the prospect of an easy meal. Glasson basin is locally important as a wintering site for diving ducks, including pochard, tufted duck, goldeneye and goosander. Cormorant also occur there in large numbers. Swallows and martins are summer visitors in many areas and can be seen flying low over the water where they feed on flying insects. You may see heron flying along or silently waiting in the shallows and, if you are lucky, you will catch the sudden bright turquoise flash of a kingfisher as it dips.

The hedges that border the more open sections of the towpath support a good variety of finches, tits and warblers. In adjacent fields expect to see and hear lapwing, skylark, pipit and buntings. In the wooded cuttings there are blackbirds, song thrushes, wrens, blackcaps, goldcrests and wood pigeons.

The summer wild flowers attract a number of butterflies, including meadow brown, speckled wood, small tortoise-shell, red admiral, peacock and the common blue. Dragonflies and the smaller damselflies can be seen darting about or basking in the sun. Watch the surface of the water for the long legged pond skater and the small whirligig beetle, which are supported by the surface tension.

Small mammals such as shrews, bank voles and water voles live in the banks, but these are shy; the best chance you may have of seeing one is from the window of a moored boat when it doesn't know you are watching! Larger mammals such as deer and fox have been seen using the well-vegetated canal banks to move from one area to another. The various structures and retaining walls of bridges, aqueducts and buildings are full of cracks, crevices and voids, which provide roosting sites for several species of bat, and an abundance of aerial insects provides a rich food supply for them.

Remember to bring along your wild flower and bird books if you are interested in identifying the hundreds of different species that enjoy living here, and please always follow the Country Code.

THE FUTURE FOR THE CANAL

The Northern Reaches Restoration

When completed this will see the 14 miles of the canal from Tewitfield to Kendal restored to navigation. It is being managed by the Lancaster Canal Regeneration Partnership – LCRP (see advert for contact and other details). This brings together the resources of not only the major national and local bodies involved with canal restoration but all the relevant local authorities and other interest groups. Significant planning progress was made a few years ago resulting in a 3-phase Plan to complete the restoration. Unfortunately implementation of Phase 1, starting from Canal Head, Kendal was thwarted by events outside LCRP control. There are significant moves to re-invigorate restoration plans, the first of which is the development of a Towpath Trail along the canal route.

Although the obstacles remain largely the same, engineering standards and techniques as well as environmental standards etc. have changed, so all the original proposals need to be re-visited, in particular the phasing.

From the south the first obstacle is crossing the A6070 at Tewitfield (formerly Br139) where there will be either a new culvert or diversion alongside the M6. Next is the Tewitfield flight of 8 locks which appear to be in reasonable condition and restoration will be fairly 'standard'. At Cinderbarrow (Br141A) the canal goes under the M6 in a culvert which is not high enough for boats to use. There are a number of options for restoration including: 1. creating a culvert at low level and moving the top lock west of the M6; 2. creating a drop lock; 3. building an aqueduct over with 'deep' locks at each end. Any works involving the M6 will be problematic and expensive. Holme North Road (Br153a) will require some realignment and a bridge over the canal. Next

Spinney Culvert also requires a culvert and might require a diversion along the M6 to gain more height over the culvert. New culverts will be required to cross the A65 at Moss Side (Br162) and Millness (Br163a).

The canal itself, up to Millness has been running at a low level since the culverting and lengths may have to be reinforced. From Millness to Stainton (Br172) the length is navigable and has been recently dredged. North of Stainton the canal was closed, drained and the land sold off. Fortunately the length is protected from development and most of the bridges are still in place and in good condition.

The length from Br172 to Wellheads Lane (before the demolished Br174) is being restored by the Lancaster Canal Trust with the generous support of the owner. The first length to Br173, the 'First Furlong' has been excavated and is currently being re-watered and tested for leakage, after which the next 400m or so, which has little in-fill will be tackled. The next obstacle is to cross the A590, the original proposal was for a culvert under but there is a possibility of using the current underpass (Wellheads Lane) for the canal and diverting the lane.

Immediately north is Hincaster Tunnel which is in good condition, and the next main problem is to cross the A590 (again) where the line of the canal as well as Br176 was totally obliterated. This will probably involve an aqueduct over the road, an impressive 'Gateway to the Lakes' for both cars and boats.

Br183 Natland Road, on the outskirts of Kendal, was demolished to straighten the road so a new bridge, slightly to the north, will be required, with an associated canal route diversion. The length south of Natland Mill Bridge (Br184) is problematic in that land was sold off and there is now only a narrow path between gardens on one side and a drop on the other. One solution is for a minimum width 'aqueduct' at ground level. It is thought that the original Highgate Settlings Bridge (Br185) is still in situ below the A65 (Burton Road) after the latter was widened. The Parkside Road crossing (not numbered) presents problems as the old bridge was removed and the road was levelled. The original proposal was for a lifting bridge but this would probably not be acceptable on a fairly busy road, an alternative is a drop lock.

The situation at Canal Head is not clear, half the basin is covered by a factory and plans to commercialise the area have stalled. Land is currently used as a council depot and a recycling facility, although there are plans to move. There is an area of land short of Canal Head that has been offered as a mooring area.

Whilst remaining committed to supporting LCRP the Trust continues to carry out minor (but necessary) maintenance work on heritage structures along the canal as well as the never ending management of trees and vegetation. This work is done by volunteers from the Trust, assisted at times by the Waterway Recovery Group and other volunteers.

The completion of the project is still some years away and it is vital to maintain public awareness and support. Readers of this book can help in this by becoming members of the Lancaster Canal Trust, hopefully as active volunteers so we are able to leave others in no doubt as to the support for this project.

Preston City Link

The Preston City Link Canal Trust was formed in 2003, the aim being to restore about ¾ mile of the filled-in section of the Lancaster Canal from its present southern terminus in Ashton to a proposed new marina in the Maudland area, near to the University of Central Lancashire. Despite an encouraging pre-feasibility study and a public exhibition of the plans and model at the Preston Minster in 2006, the scheme lacked adequate support and the Preston City Link Canal Trust was wound up in 2012.

CRUISING THE LANCASTER CANAL

The main line of the canal offers 41 miles of relaxing, lock-free boating and for the more energetic there are the six locks down to Glasson Basin. The absence of locks on the main line means that the majority of the canal is available for cruising all year round. Sections are occasionally closed in the winter as publicised in the Canal & River Trust national stoppage programme. If in doubt contact C&RT on their dedicated Twitter feed @CRTnotices, directly on 0303 040 4040, or www.canalrivertrust.org.uk. North of Tewitfield there are opportunities for using canoes and dinghies on some of the disjointed sections. A C&RT licence is required for all craft using the canal. Members of the British Canoe Union are licensed through BCU membership; others should contact C&RT. Trail boats can be launched at Millness, between bridges 163a & 164, on a 2½ mile section to Stainton. Contact the Canal & River Trust (see p.92) for arrangements to use the slipway.

Mooring: the Canal & River Trust provide approved visitor moorings with facilities for rubbish disposal etc. and these should be used where possible. Do not moor longer than necessary at water points or sanitary stations. In theory you can moor anywhere on the towpath side unless there is specific indication to the contrary. However, in places bankside vegetation can extend several feet into the channel and care must be exercised when mooring away from established sites. Some of the locations where towpath mooring is feasible for most craft are marked on the maps with an anchor symbol. Many people find mooring near overhead power lines disturbing; there are many locations where lines cross or run close to the canal and the principal ones are marked on the maps. The canal was built as a barge waterway – the channel cross section is a shallow 'V'– and skippers of narrow boats and craft with a deep draft may find it difficult to get close in to the bank and may need to use a plank for access. Do not moor where your boat is a hazard to navigation, such as at bends, junctions or locks. Approach the bank slowly, front first, at a slight angle and allow a member of the crew to step off the boat. Put the engine in neutral and pull the back of the boat in with your rope. The boat must be tied up at the front and back but never tie ropes across the towing path where they could be a hazard to walkers and other users. When leaving, push the boat away from the bank before engaging the engine, to prevent the propeller damaging the bed of the canal or itself.

On the Move: You should keep to the centre of the channel but move over to the right when meeting oncoming boats and pass left to left. Overtake on the left. On some of the shallower sections it is possible to run aground near the edges. You should be able to simply reverse off but may have to use a boat pole, making sure the crew is well away from where the boat is stuck. The official speed limit is 4 mph, a fast walking pace. However, if your wash breaks on the bank, you are going too fast, using more fuel than you need, and more importantly you will also be causing damage to the canal banks. In shallow water, boats will actually travel faster if you reduce engine speed, because over-revving pulls the bottom of the boat deeper into the water. Do not overtake on a bend, near a bridge, lock or where you cannot see the way ahead. Slow down when being overtaken so as still to have steerage way. Slow down when passing anglers, moored boats, other moving craft or repair works. Please do not disturb the peace of the waterway by playing radios, stereos or televisions too loud.

Locks: If you are hiring a boat for the first time ensure the boatyard gives you adequate instruction but remember the following points. Where possible share locks with boats travelling in the same direction. If there is a boat coming in the opposite direction and the lock is in their favour i.e. you would need to either fill or empty it first, then wait for them to pass through. This saves water and some effort on your part. When leaving a lock always ensure that all the paddles are down and the gates are closed, unless there is a boat approaching from the opposite direction when it is courteous to leave the gates open for them. Obey all instructions for the use of locks provided by the Canal & River Trust or its staff.

The **maximum dimensions** for cruising craft are:

Main Line
Length	72 feet / 22 m.
Width	14 feet / 4.26 m.
Headroom (Br. 129b)	8 feet / 2.4 m.
(except Ashton Basin	*6ft 10ins / 2.1 m.)*
Draught	3 feet / 0.9 m.

Glasson Branch
Length	70 feet / 21.3 m.
Width	14 feet / 4.26 m.
Headroom	8 feet / 2.4 m.

Millennium Ribble Link
Length	62 feet / 18.9 m.
Width	10ft 6ins / 3.2 m.
Headroom	8 feet / 2.4 m.
Draught	2ft / 0.6 m.

Length, width and draught clearances on the Link are inter-related, full details are available from the Canal & River Trust.

Some of the boat hire establishments on the Lancaster Canal do not allow their boats to use the Glasson Branch locks. Instead, a circular walk from the visitor moorings at Galgate will take you down the branch to Glasson Dock and back via a series of footpaths and minor roads.

Services: There are sanitary stations at Cadley, Bilsborrow, Garstang, Galgate, Lancaster, Carnforth, and Tewitfield. All service stations require a C&RT Yale key for access. The Yale key is standard throughout the canal system. Prepay cards are required for the use of pump outs and are available from marinas and chandleries on the Lancaster Canal and from C&RT (see p.92). Electric hook-ups at the Glasson Basin visitor moorings use the same prepay cards but also require a security key available on loan (deposit required) from the C&RT.

The service stations at Galgate and Glasson Basin are operated by British Waterways Marinas Ltd (BWML). They need the same C&RT Yale key for access but a different prepay card for pumpout, available only from BWML at these Marinas.

FISHING THE CANAL

Angling is permitted from the towpath side on both the cruising and remainder sections between Preston and Stainton. The main fish species are roach, perch and bream, with smaller numbers of pike, tench, carp, gudgeon and chub. Eel occur throughout the canal. The best fishing areas are the rural stretches between Preston and Lancaster, particularly on the Glasson Branch. There is also good fishing on the Northern Reaches above Tewitfield and on the rural stretches north of Carnforth. Rod licences must be obtained from the Environment Agency. Fishing rights to various stretches of the canal belong to local angling clubs and the Waterways Wanderers Scheme also gives rights to other stretches of canal fishing. Information is available at: www.canalrivertrust.org.uk/enjoy-the-waterways/fishing – or email fisheries@canalrivertrust.org.uk.

The Lancaster Canal is an important leisure area for boaters, cyclists and walkers as well as anglers so please observe the following code of conduct:

- Do not obstruct the towing path.
- Always take litter home and light no fires.
- Take care near power lines; there are many that cross or run close to the canal.
- When a boat approaches, lift your rod and line to one side.
- Do not fish at locks, bridge holes or from landing stages.

Further information may be obtained from local tackle shops or by contacting the Canal & River Trust (see p.92).

WALKING THE CANAL

The use of the towpath by walkers is actively encouraged despite the fact that much of it is not a public right of way. Access points are numerous and there are many fingerposts and waymark boards to show the way. It provides easy level walking throughout its entire length in mainly rural surroundings. It is mostly grass, generally wide and in good condition, though it can be muddy during winter months and after wet weather, particularly in Salwick and Ashton Road cuttings. There is a good smooth hard surfaced towpath for the first two miles in Preston as far as Bridge 17, again through Garstang (Br.58-64) and the ten miles from Ashton Road, Lancaster (Br.94) to Carnforth (Br.129), plus other short lengths. Further towpath improvements are in hand.

North of Tewitfield the towpath continues all the way to Canal Head in Kendal, the section in Cumbria being a definitive public footpath. Several short diversions are necessary due to road crossings, but these are either obvious or indicated by LCT signposts. The towpath as far as Stainton (the northern limit of the watered section) is in excellent condition, but beyond here the route of the canal is in various ownerships and is less well maintained, though still easily passable. From Sedgwick into Kendal much

of the channel has been infilled but the line of the former towpath is obvious, although there are obstacles in the form of stiles and gates.

The opening of a footpath along much of the line of the Millennium Ribble Link now offers a fine long distance circular walk utilising the Lancashire Coastal Way. This waymarked route follows the shoreline of Lancashire as closely as possible from Southport to the border of Cumbria near Arnside using existing footpaths and other highways. Near lock 8 on the Link a footpath leads to Blackpool Road from where the coastal route can be joined. A shorter circuit leaves the Link at lock 7, joins the minor road from Lea Town to Br 18 on the main canal and follows the towpath back to the top of the Link.

Many walks can be combined with a bus journey to start or finish. Bus stops close to the canal are marked on the maps and a table of bus routes can be found on p.89. There is endless scope for circular walks using the towpath and the numerous footpaths and bridle paths that cross the canal bridges. There are several books describing walks on and around the canal. A book list can be found on p.91. The county and district councils have also published leaflets about walks in their areas. This information is generally available from the various Tourist Information Centres listed on p.91.

Enjoy walking in safety and observe the following code of conduct:
- Wear stout shoes (boots in winter) and take a waterproof.
- Keep away from the canal edge and make sure that children are supervised.
- Always follow the Country Code.
- Obey the Canal & River Trust by-laws and share the towpath with consideration for other users.

Access for All. Generally speaking those lengths of towpath identified as suitable for cycling (see next section) are suitable for wheelchairs and buggies and those with limited mobility. They have easy access points and a good smooth surface. There is also a stretch of good towpath through Garstang. Step-free access points are shown on the maps. The Canal & River Trust is working towards improving waterways access and have an 'access for all' policy. The improved towpath between Lancaster and Carnforth forms part of this policy. More specific information is available from C&RT (see p.92).

The Lancaster Canal Regeneration Partnership is promoting the Towpath Trail Project which aims to construct and promote a multi-user pathway along the line of the canal initially between Kendal and Lancaster but, in the longer term, onwards to Preston.

CYCLING ON THE CANAL

Several lengths of the canal have been designated as suitable for use by bicycles, these being:

Preston – from Ashton Basin to Br.17 Cottam Hall – approx 2 miles – part of the National Cycle Route Network.

Millennium Ribble Link – from Lock 8 to the canal junction near Br.16 – approx 2 miles forms part of the 'Guild Wheel'.

Lancaster to Carnforth, Br.94 Ashton Road to ¼ mile past Br.129 Hodgsons – approx 10 miles, much of which forms part of the National Cycle Route Network.

In **Kendal** the infilled canal between Natland Road and Canal Head is a shared use path for walkers and cyclists.

These sections all have a good hard surfaced towpath, whereas on other parts of the canal cycling is not encouraged because of the poorer condition of the towpath and the risk of damaging it in wet conditions.

Cycle with care at all times and show consideration for other towpath users. Take extra care under bridges. Visitors bringing a cycle with them will find it a useful form of transport for exploring some beautiful parts of Lancashire and Cumbria, especially in conjunction with the Ordnance Survey maps covering the area. If you cannot bring your own, you can hire cycles in **Lancaster** and **Morecambe**, see list on p.90.

The Guild Wheel, a 21 mile circular cycle route round Preston to celebrate the 2012 Preston Guild, runs along part of the Ribble Link Canal. Other highlights of the Guild Wheel are the route along the River Ribble from Brockholes Nature Reserve to Preston Dock. You can cycle and walk along the Old Tramroad south from Avenham Park by the river in the centre of Preston. You can continue on cycle route 55 to Chorley where you can join the Leeds and Liverpool Canal to Adlington.

The northern section of the Lancashire Cycleway (Route 90) provides a loop consisting of 130 miles of waymarked route taking in the Fylde plain, north to Lancaster and the Arnside/ Silverdale area before returning south through the Pennines and Forest of Bowland. The route crosses the canal at Bridges 26, 36, 44, 79, 128 and 141.

From Lancaster there are three off-road routes; one to Glasson Dock, the second running eastwards alongside the River Lune to Caton and beyond and the third connecting to Morecambe and Heysham, all utilising former railways for much of their length. In Morecambe a route continues northwards along the promenade, linking to the canal towpath via Rushley Drive, giving a circular route of about 11 miles.

The Way of Roses Cycleway from Morecambe to Bridlington runs beneath the Lune Aqueduct along the River Lune Millennium Park cycle path.

The Bay Cycle Way, Route 700 opened in 2015 and links Walney Island, Barrow-in-Furness to Glasson Dock via the Morecambe Bay coastline and uses the Lancaster Canal towpath between Carnforth and Bolton-le-Sands.

For further information on cycle routes in the area see:
www.lancashire.gov.uk/cycling and
www.sustrans.org.uk

ABOUT THE LANCASTER CANAL TRUST

When the Lancaster Canal Trust was formed in 1963, its prime objective was to restore and re-open to navigation, the disused section of the canal from Tewitfield to Kendal. These plans were soon thwarted by the Ministry of Transport's proposals for the northward extension of the M6 motorway, involving several crossings of the canal by culvert, rather than by bridge. It is fortunate that the canal's engineer, John Rennie, chose a site as far north as Crooklands as the entry point for the canal's water supply from Killington Reservoir, otherwise it is unlikely any of the canal north of Tewitfield would have survived at all! Despite a six year battle, the Ministry finally won the day. The far-sightedness displayed by the Trust was not shared by the Ministry. The commercial traffic on the canal had long since finished and few pleasure craft used the waterway. Not many people at that time envisaged the coming of the second 'canal age', the boom in leisure use and the great interest in protection and restoration of the canal system.

Despite these setbacks, the main objective of the Trust is still the restoration of the canal to Kendal, though the task is immensely greater now than it was in 1963. The Trust has joined with the local authorities, Canal & River Trust and other interest groups in the Lancaster Canal Regeneration Partnership, a steering group to drive the project forward and realise this goal.

In addition, the Trust supports the development of the whole of the canal as a public amenity while at the same time seeking to protect its essential character. The Trust works with Canal & River Trust and with the various county, city and district councils to extend and improve facilities available to users. We maintain a watching brief on developments near the canal and are regularly consulted on planning applications submitted to the 5 district councils through whose areas the canal passes.

Over the years, as a result of the efforts of the Trust, many of the original structures have been given statutory protection either as listed structures or scheduled ancient monuments. Further losses of cruising waterway have been successfully resisted, notably in Preston. The Trust has funded many improvements along the towpath, with information & interpretive panels, benches and fingerposts provided at various sites. Through our membership of the Lancaster Canal Regeneration Partnership, the Trust actively supports the Towpath Trail project which aims to construct and promote a mult-user pathway along the line of the canal. The trail will initially be between Kendal and Lancaster but, in the longer term, onward to Preston. We also work in conjunction with other bodies representing the variety of canal users, many of which are affiliated to the Trust. The Trust itself is a Corporate Member of the Inland Waterways Association and is a registered charity.

The Trust actively supported the work of the Ribble Link Trust in its successful mission to link the Lancaster Canal to the main canal network via the River Ribble. In 2012 the Trust welcomed the IWA National Campaign Festival to the Lancaster Canal as part of the Preston Guild celebrations.

Every Sunday and Bank Holiday Monday from the beginning of May to the end of September the Trust runs public boat trips from Crooklands (Br.166) in a purpose built 28ft narrow boat, Waterwitch. The boat is also available for charter trips for schools, clubs and private parties. There are regular working parties carrying out maintenance and improvement projects on footpaths, steps, bridges, locks, etc. and from time to time more major tasks have been undertaken in conjunction with the Waterway Recovery Group. The Trust's marquee is frequently seen at national waterways events and at a variety of regional shows, with a dedicated team of volunteers and a range of sales and promotional material. A panel of speakers is available to talk to public meetings and to local clubs and societies with a PowerPoint presentation about the canal. The Trust's magazine, 'Waterwitch' includes news, feature articles, photos and other matters of interest. And of course this guide book is the tangible result of the Trust's activities and our desire to share our enthusiasm for this splendid canal.

All these activities are covered in more detail on the Lancaster Canal Trust's website, www.lctrust.co.uk, which is frequently up-dated.

We need your help to enable the Trust to achieve its aims and objectives, particularly the goal of re-opening the canal to Kendal. If you enjoy the Lancaster Canal, please think about joining the Trust. Membership details can be found below.

The Lancaster Canal Trust would like to thank all the contributors to this Guide and hopes that the value of this publication will be appreciated by all users of the Canal, both on and off the water. We are grateful to our advertisers for their contributions towards the production costs of this book.

For information about membership of the Lancaster Canal Trust please contact:
Membership Secretary, Lancaster Canal Trust, c/o Lancaster District CVS, Sulyard Street, Lancaster LA1 1PX

Or visit www.lctrust.co.uk for a membership application form.

MAP OF THE LANCASTER CANAL

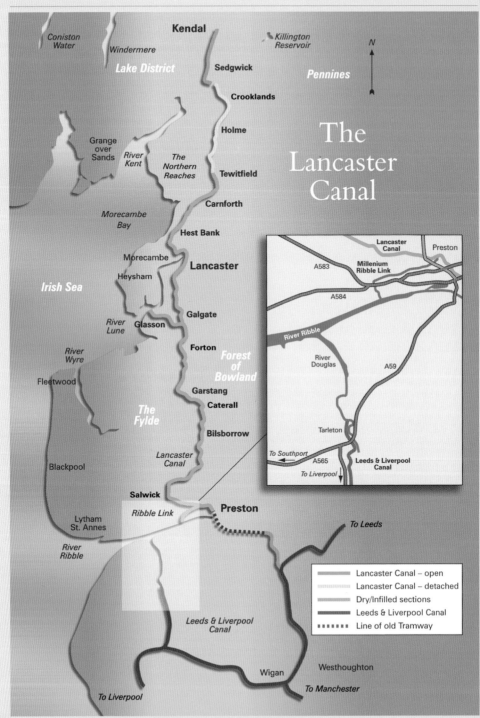

Coniston Water

Windermere

Kendal

Killington Reservoir

Lake District

Sedgwick

Pennines

Crooklands

N

Holme

Grange over Sands

River Kent

The Northern Reaches

Tewitfield

The
Lancaster
Canal

Carnforth

Morecambe Bay

Hest Bank

Morecambe

Heysham

Lancaster

Irish Sea

Galgate

River Lune

Glasson

Forton

Forest of Bowland

River Wyre

Garstang

Fleetwood

Caterall

The Fylde

Bilsborrow

Lancaster Canal

Blackpool

Salwick

Lytham St. Annes

Ribble Link

Preston

River Ribble

To Leeds

Leeds & Liverpool Canal

Wigan

Westhoughton

To Liverpool

To Manchester

Lancaster Canal

Preston

A583

Millenium Ribble Link

A584

River Ribble

River Douglas

A59

Tarleton

To Southport

A565

Leeds & Liverpool Canal

To Liverpool

	Lancaster Canal – open
	Lancaster Canal – detached
	Dry/Infilled sections
	Leeds & Liverpool Canal
	Line of old Tramway

INFORMATION AND KEY

Key to map symbols
(This key can also be found on the back flap)

Facilities
* ❋ Boat Yard
* ♙ Calor Gas
* ⓒ Coal
* ⓞ Diesel
* ♟ Elsan
* ⓟ Pumpout
* ♟ Refuse/Recycling
* ⚒ Water
* ⒲ WC
* ⓐ Laundry
* ⚓ Chandlery / Shop
* ♝ Shower
* ⚞ Slipway/Crane
* ⚒ Repairs
* ⚓ Narrow Boat Hire
* ⚓ Day Boat Hire
* ♟ Visitor Moorings
* ⤳ Other good Moorings
* ⦿ Winding Hole
* ⌒ Coke Oven

General
* ⛽ Petrol Station
* ⛩ General Store
* ⛃ Pub
* ⒫ PO
* ⒤ Info
* ✆ Telephone
* ⇌ Station
* ☕ Café Tearoom
* ● Bus stop

◀ Canal with towpath

Access to towpath:
* Ⓛ Level Path
* Ⓡ Ramp
* Ⓢ Steps
* Ⓖ Gate/Chicane
* sⓣ Stile

⑧③ Bridge, number & name

▬ A Road

▬ B Road

Other Roads*

Footpath*

Tracks/Drives*

Bridleway*

Cycle path

❋ Named Marina

Ⓢ Sanitary Station

Aqueduct /other watercourse

Lock

⦿ Winding hole

⑪ Mile post
㊺ Mileage to Kendal – *upper figure* (Canal Head) and from Preston – *lower figure* (Original City Centre Basin)

◀ Canal no longer in water or in-filled

✕━━✕ Overhead power lines

* *The inclusion of roads and paths in this guide does not automatically indicate a public right of way*

Cruising Times
The table shows approximate cruising times in hours and minutes between principal locations.

It is based on the maximum permitted speed of 4 miles per hour but with an allowance for slowing down when passing moored boats, meeting another boat at a bridge etc.

Tewitfield										
1.10	Carnforth									
2.10	1.00	Hest Bank								
3.25	2.20	1.20	Lancaster							
4.45	3.35	2.35	1.20	Galgate						
5.35	4.25	3.25	2.10	0.55	Forton					
7.00	5.55	4.55	3.35	2.20	1.25	Garstang				
8.25	7.20	6.20	5.00	3.45	2.55	1.25	Bilsborrow			
9.55	8.45	7.45	6.25	5.10	4.20	2.55	1.25	Catforth		
10.25	9.20	8.20	7.00	5.45	4.55	3.25	2.00	0.35	Salwick	
11.45	10.35	9.35	8.20	7.00	6.10	4.45	3.20	1.55	1.20	Preston

THE RIBBLE LINK

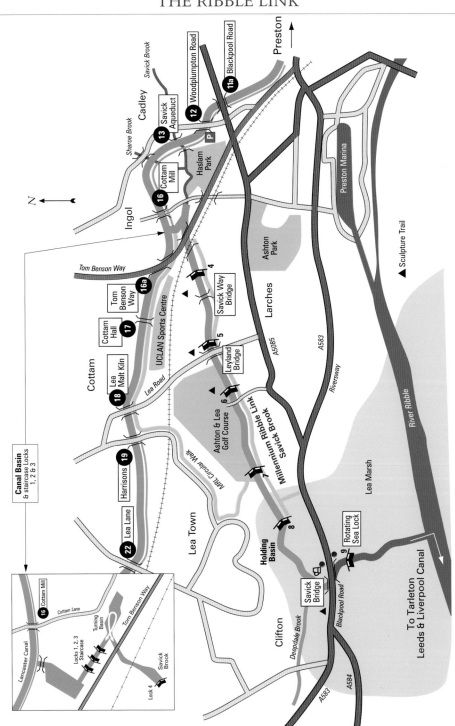

THE MILLENNIUM RIBBLE LINK

About the Ribble Link

The Millennium Ribble Link is the first new navigation to be constructed in England since the Manchester Ship Canal. Built purely for recreation and leisure at a cost of £5.8m, the Link was opened in 2002. It connects the Lancaster Canal to the estuary of the River Ribble and via its tributary, the River Douglas, to the existing sea lock at Tarleton on the Rufford Branch of the Leeds & Liverpool Canal.

The Link has nine locks. The sea lock is a 'rising sector gate' which is lowered into the river bed during operation and raised to impound the water as the tide goes out. Locks 8 to 4 control the levels and straighten many of the bends of Savick Brook to make it navigable. A three-chambered staircase lock leads into the top basin at the junction with the Lancaster canal between bridges 16 and 16a.

In canalising Savick Brook care was taken to retain the original north bank; this has conserved the existing flora and fauna. The south bank was re-colonised quickly following the construction work. Two sides of the top mooring basin have been gently sloped to create a natural environment and much of the Link is a wildlife and wildflower preserve. The fish passes which have been constructed are of innovative design and were developed in partnership with the Environment Agency.

A footpath, cycleway and nature trail runs alongside the Link down to Lock 8. From this point a short length of footpath connects to Blackpool Road (A583). The staircase locks 1–3 and Lock 8 are proving to be attractive locations for visitors wanting to see boats using the Link. Access points for disabled and less mobile people are plentiful and operational staff may be on hand to provide assistance.

A sculpture trail called 'Gauging the Ripple' has been commissioned along the Link. This project has attracted a great deal of interest, with five pieces by sculptor Thompson Dagnall. Other enhancement works include an outdoor classroom at Ashton Primary School, a hay meadow to provide a haven for wildflowers and insects and the installation of various benches along the Link. All this has been achieved with the help of funding from The Millennium Commission, Arts Council, Awards for All, The Waterways Trust and British Waterways.

Navigating the Ribble Link

The Link is owned and operated by the Canal & River Trust. The Link connects to the Lancaster Canal between bridges 16 & 16a where there is a mooring basin for assembly of convoys down the Link. Staircase locks 1–3 are operated by the Canal & River Trust staff. Locks 4–8 on Savick Brook are operated by boat crews themselves. Lock 9, the sea lock, is also controlled by C&RT staff.. Passage through the link is continuous, though in emergency boats may be required to moor at Lock 8.

Below Lock 9 the last ½ mile of the Savick Brook runs into the River Ribble. Access upriver is to Preston Marina or downriver to the River Douglas and Tarleton Lock, connecting into the Rufford Branch of the Leeds & Liverpool Canal

The link will be operational on as many days as possible between Easter and the end of October, when the following conditions are met:

- a tide level of 8.5 – 9.6 metres,
- suitable fresh water flow in Savick Brook,
- winds up to Beaufort scale 4/5,
- in daylight hours and good visibility,
- one direction only on any one day.

The Canal & River Trust has the right to cancel operation on the day if conditions are not suitable.

There is no charge for long term licence holders; for those with less than a 3-month licence there is a charge of £60 for a return journey. All passages must be pre-booked via the Canal and River Trust website. Further information on navigating the Ribble Link including operating dates and times is also available on the website. A copy of the Skipper's Guide can be downloaded from the Canal and River Trust website: www.canalrivertrust.org.uk

PRESTON

Preston was granted City status in 2002. It was the coming of the canal, quickly followed by the railway, which transformed Preston from a market town into an industrial town and port, particularly important during the boom years of the Lancashire cotton industry. This resulted in the town being completely remodelled and none of the buildings is more than 200 years old. Preston's growth was such that it eclipsed Lancaster, the old county town and it is now the administrative centre for Lancashire. The cotton magnates bequeathed many fine buildings, notably the Town Hall and the Harris Library & Museum, located on the Flag Market. Also of note is the Guildhall, a modern building containing the Charter Theatre.

The shopping area contains all the usual high street names plus a wide variety of eating and drinking establishments catering for all tastes, while the town still retains its past in the open and covered markets. The majority of shops are located along Fishergate and in the Fishergate and St George's Centres. Just off Fishergate can be found Winckley Square a fine collection of Georgian and Edwardian property. Now mostly used commercially, this was the place to live for Preston's gentry, and it is not difficult to imagine how life must have been in Victorian times. Just beyond, to the south, lie the two gems of Preston's many parks, Avenham and Miller Parks, with wide open expanses sweeping down to the River Ribble. The parks are well worth a visit if only to trace the route of the tramroad and to view the replica bridge that carried it across the Ribble.

The Canal now starts a mile or so north west of the City centre at Ashton Basin.

From Ashton Basin buses run frequently into the city. All services from this area start and terminate at the bus station and are operated mainly by Preston Bus – have plenty of small change available as change is not given on these buses. The bus station is a short walk from Lancaster Road and the Harris Museum, through St John's shopping centre. The tourist information centre is located on Lancaster Road at the entrance to the Guildhall complex.

THE CANAL FROM PRESTON • 10 – 19

The Lancaster Canal commences at Aqueduct Street near its junction with Fylde Road, a mile or so north west of Preston City centre. Pedestrian access to the towpath is by one of two footpaths – one near the bottom of Shelley Road and the other from Aqueduct Street itself (between the A.T.S. Tyre Specialist and Kirkham Funerals). A finger signpost indicates Catforth 7 miles, Garstang 16¼, Tewitfield (cruising terminus) 41¼, Kendal 57, Dalesway 60 and (in the other direction) Preston Town Centre ½ mile, Harris Museum ½ mile. Road access to Ashton Basin (approximately 250 yards from the southern end of the canal) is from the mini roundabout 50 yards from the bottom of Tulketh Brow near Wycliffe Memorial Church on an unmarked, unpaved entrance. The adjacent entrance gives access to the canal towpath. Full length boats can turn close to the end of the canal by using the entrance to Ashton Basin. The next half mile of canal lies in a cutting surrounded on both sides by housing. Woodplumpton Road crosses the canal at Bridge 12, from where a short walk on the towpath side leads to shops at Lane Ends and buses to Preston centre and Blackpool. After Bridge 12 Haslam Park opens up on the left offering pleasant walking, municipal bowling greens and tennis courts and a large children's play area. On the right, on the site of a former coal wharf, are Cadley sanitary station, a few 7-day visitor moorings and a picnic and barbecue area.

Bridge 13 is the first aqueduct on the canal, where Savick Brook flows under the canal, through Haslam Park and becomes the basis for the Millennium Ribble Link. Bridge 14, Hollinghead Fold, is the first of many of Rennie's standard masonry arch bridges spanning the canal. The canal now swings westward around the park. Bridge 15, Ingol Ashes, has a pointed parapet rather than a curved one and it is topped with rails. The next bridge, Cottam Mill, is similar but without rails. After Bridge 16 a sign warns of craft entering from the towpath side where the Millennium Ribble Link canal connects with the Lancaster Canal, providing access to the Leeds Liverpool Canal and the rest of the inland waterway network. (see page 29). Just after Bridge 16a is the UCLan Sports Arena (Tel: 01772 761000), which provides pitches and courts for most sports, together with changing facilities, etc. The Arena extends almost to Bridge 18. The main entrance to the Arena for boaters is at Bridge 17 where mooring is provided. Bridge 17, Cottam Hall, is a skew Rennie standard – not a common type on the Lancaster Canal as most are at 90 degrees to the water channel. Between Bridges 16a and 18 at Cottam landscaped areas around the housing on the right of the canal include a canalside walk, small children's play area and a pier with a signpost stating Lancaster Canal: Preston 2½ miles, Tewitfield 40 miles. Lea Road crosses the canal at Bridge 18 – Lea Malt Kiln Bridge. The houses finally peter out and beyond lies open countryside with the railway line nearby to the south.

National Cycle Route 62 follows the towpath from the end of the canal at Shelley Road as far as Cottam Hall Bridge (17), with access points near bridges 10, 14, 15, 16 and at Haslam Park.

THE CANAL FROM
PRESTON Bridges 10 – 19

MARINAS/BOATHIRE
Arlen Hire Boats, Ashton Basin, Br.10. ⚓🛥️🌀🅾️🛒🚤
Tel: 01772 769183 www.arlen-hireboats.co.uk

FOOD
SPAR, Woodplumpton Rd. 250yd W of Br.11a.
Tel 01772 726541

PUBS
There are numerous pubs in Preston, the following can be found close to the canal.

Lane's End, Blackpool Road, 250yds W of Br.11a. Tel 01772 733362

The Ancient Oak, Merrytrees Lane, Cottam, 1 mile N of Br.17. Tel: 01772 731992

Saddle Inn, Bartle. ¾ mile N of Br.19. SD 486 327. Tel: 01772 726616

Sitting Goose, Bartle. 1 mile N of Br.19. SD 486 330. Tel: 01772 690344

ATTRACTIONS
The City of Preston is home to a number of museums with exhibitions and activities for the whole family. There is a good selection of shops and a choice of multiplex cinemas.

Harris Museum & Art Gallery, Discover Preston History Gallery, fine & decorative arts, temporary exhibitions programme, café, shop. Free admission, open daily except BH. Tel: 01772 258248 www.harrismuseum.org.uk

Lancashire Infantry Museum, (formerly the Queen's Lancashire Regiment Museum) Fulwood Barracks. Free admission (ID required), open Tuesday, Thursday & Saturday. Tel: 01772 260584

UCLan Sports Arena, Tom Benson Way, canalside Br 16a – 17. Tel 01772 761000

Access to towpath
KEY
L Level Path
R Ramp
S Steps
G Gate/Chicane
sT Stile

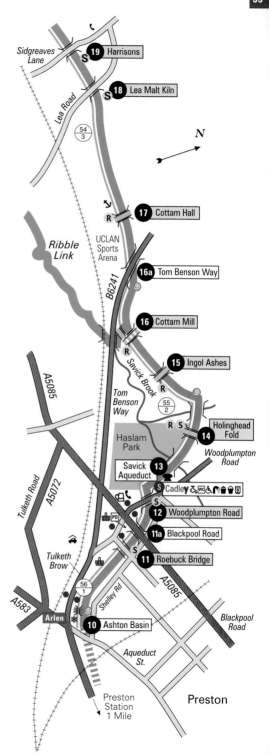

SALWICK • 20 – 32

The canal continues westwards through open country, with the railway in close proximity. The only intrusion on an otherwise rural landscape is the Springfields plant of BNFL/Westinghouse, which manufactures fuel rods for nuclear power stations. The former Lea Swing Bridge (20) has been removed with hardly a trace left. The small cluster of buildings on the left is Lea Town which has a pub that can be reached from Bridge 22. As you approach Bridge 24, the canal swings north, passing Salwick Hall (private) on the right. The canal from Bridge 19 to 25 is within the BNFL/Westinghouse emergency zone; if you hear a loud continuous siren – leave the area as quickly as possible. There is a warning notice at Bridge 25. From Bridge 25 it is a short walk to Salwick Station and just beyond Bridge 25 lies Salwick Wharf which once served the market town of Kirkham and is now a popular mooring spot. The great loop that the canal traverses was made to accommodate a projected canal to Fleetwood. Past Salwick Wharf, the next half mile is in a cutting lined with mature trees of various species, especially notable for the autumn colours of the beeches. Marshalls Bridge (27) is also known as Six Mile Bridge and a nearby milestone indicates that on original mileage, you are now six miles from Preston.

Salwick Moss Bridge (28) used to be nicknamed New Bridge, because it replaced a former lift bridge. The canal heads due north, passing under the M55 motorway. From Bridge 29 a fine view west across the rural Fylde plain can be seen, the most striking feature being the many radio masts of RNWS Inskip, a communications centre for the Ministry of Defence. Just south of Bridge 32 is a water point and on the north side there is a boatyard housed in the old canal cottages and stables. Visitor moorings 150yds north of Bridge 32, though boaters may find overnight noise from the M55 intrusive.

SALWICK **Bridges 20 – 32**

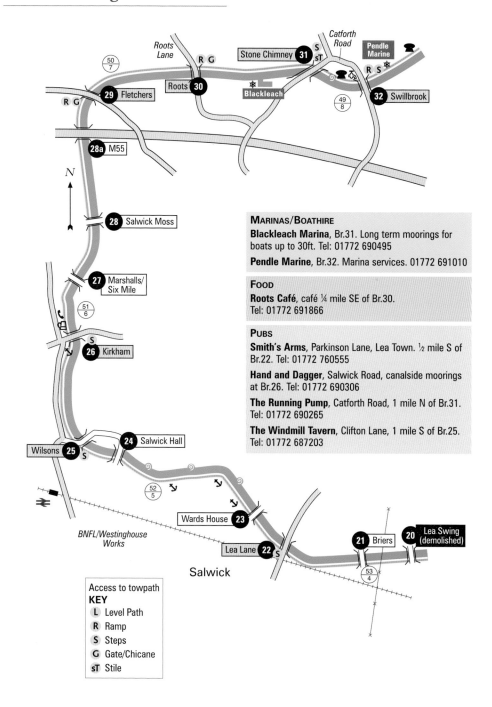

MARINAS/BOATHIRE
Blackleach Marina, Br.31. Long term moorings for boats up to 30ft. Tel: 01772 690495
Pendle Marine, Br.32. Marina services. 01772 691010

FOOD
Roots Café, café ¼ mile SE of Br.30.
Tel: 01772 691866

PUBS
Smith's Arms, Parkinson Lane, Lea Town. ½ mile S of Br.22. Tel: 01772 760555
Hand and Dagger, Salwick Road, canalside moorings at Br.26. Tel: 01772 690306
The Running Pump, Catforth Road, 1 mile N of Br.31. Tel: 01772 690265
The Windmill Tavern, Clifton Lane, 1 mile S of Br.25. Tel: 01772 687203

Access to towpath
KEY
L Level Path
R Ramp
S Steps
G Gate/Chicane
sT Stile

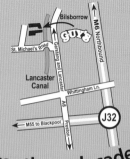
Bridge 44

BILSBORROW • 33 – 44

Bridge 33 is in fact an aqueduct carrying the canal over Woodplumpton Brook and is worth a closer look, though the only access is on the offside. There are numerous aqueducts on the canal, all designed by John Rennie. One has since been destroyed and another replaced. No two are alike and the traveller should stop and examine the larger ones as they represent fine examples of canal engineering. Woodplumpton village itself is best reached from Bridge 35 or 36. The churchyard is reputed to contain the body of a witch. This can be identified by the large boulder covering the grave so as, according to legend, to prevent the witch from digging her way out.

Bridge 37 is a swing bridge, one of only three built on this canal; leave it set as you find it, open or closed. Just beyond lies Hollowforth Mill, now a private residence, but once a water mill. Hollowforth Aqueduct (38) is an interesting three arch structure and one may walk through the northernmost arch. The canal now enters an entirely rural landscape, remote from major roads. After Bridge 39 the spire of the parish church over to the east identifies the village of Barton, a long straggling collection of houses and farms on the A6. It is just over 1 mile to the village from Bridge 39 via Station Lane, or a shorter walk by a footpath from either Bridge 40 or 41 (through Lower Park Head Farm yard). The village has a couple of pubs and a hotel. Buses run along the A6 to Preston, Garstang and Lancaster. From Bridge 42 it is a short walk to former White Horse pub on the A6 which is now an Indian restaurant. The village of Bilsborrow lies on the A6, east of Bridges 44 & 45 and is marked on some maps as Duncombe. Bilsborrow sanitary station is located here on the offside. A mile west of Bridge 44 (by road) and 45 (by footpath) lies the main campus of Myerscough College with its garden centre and cafe open to the public; (Tel: 01995 642222). Just before Bridge 45, the canal widens into a basin. 14-day visitor moorings, Bridge 44 – 45.

Woodplumpton: PO; Tel; ½ mile south of Bridge 35.

Bilsborrow: PO; Tel; Stores; Pubs. Bridge 44 – 45. A village built along the A6.

BILSBORROW **Bridges 33 – 44**

MARINAS/BOATHIRE

Moons Bridge Marina, Br.36. ☺🅾⚓🛒💺🍴🔧
Tel: 01772 690627. www.moonsbridgemarina.co.uk

Lancaster Canal Cruises, Offside between Br.44&45.
47-seat charter trip boat 'Jungle Queen' with bar,
music & PowerPoint systems, toilets. Tel: 01995
640336. www.party-boats.co.uk/www.lcccruise.co.uk

FOOD

Honeywell farm Shop, 1mile NW of Br.39. A fine
selection of locally produced meats and other produce.
Tel: 01772 690271.

Barton Bangla Brasserie, A6 Barton. ½mile E of
Br.42. Indian & Bangladeshi cuisine, M – F from
5.30pm, Sat/Sun from 1pm. Tel: 01995 640236

PUBS

Plough at Eaves, 1 mile NW of Br.39. SD 495 375.
Tel: 01772 690233

Boar's Head, A6 Barton. ¾ mile E of Br.39. SD
517 362. Tel: 01772 864330 *(being refurbished)*

The Sparling, A6 Barton. ¾ mile E of Br.39.
Tel: 01772 860830

The Walled Garden, Barton Grange Hotel, A6 Barton.
Tel: 01772 866135

Owd Nell's Tavern, Pub, Restaurant, Hotel, Tearooms,
Canalside Br.44. Tel: 01995 640010

White Bull, Offside moorings between Br.44&45,
free wi-fi. Tel: 01995 643334

Roebuck, E side of A6, Br.44. Tel: 01995 640234

Olde Duncombe Guest House, A6, Offside between
Br.44&45. B&B accommodation. Tel: 01995 640336

Access to towpath
KEY
L Level Path
R Ramp
S Steps
G Gate/Chicane
sT Stile

HOLIDAY IN FIVE STAR LUXURY...

Are you living life at full speed? Do you need to slow down and unwind? Take a relaxing holiday on Lancashire's only five-star narrowboats and see life differently

Crabtree Narrowboat Hire

There are boating holidays...and then there are unforgettable boating holidays. At Crabtree Narrowboat Hire they don't expect you to leave life's little luxuries at home. All their boats are superbly equipped with each narrowboat being assessed and awarded 5 stars by VisitEngland – the national tourist board for England. They are the only narrowboat hire company on the Lancaster Canal to have been presented with this prestigious award.

In 2015 Crabtree Narrowboat Hire were also awarded a VisitEngland ROSE Award in Recognition Of Service Excellence. This VisitEngland honor is awarded annually to only 100 VisitEngland quality assessed accommodation businesses that go the extra mile to provide excellent customer service and they are the only Narrowboat Company in the country to have been awarded this prestigious award. Owner Robert Foulkes says these awards were exactly what he set out to achieve when he launched Crabtree Narrowboat Hire. 'I

wanted to introduce top-end narrowboats onto the Lancaster Canal which offered a level of service, comfort and luxury that is normally associated with a five star hotel,' he said. Before making your booking you are welcome to take a look at the boats (if they are in!) and our hire prices include VAT, water, towels & bedding, fuel, gas, insurance and car parking.

Choose a short break, a full week or even longer and explore the tranquil and lock-free Lancaster Canal. You will soon discover that travelling at less than four miles an hour is the perfect way of slowing you down! Your biggest decision each day is either to moor by one of the waterside pubs or go off exploring the small market towns and delightful villages on your route.

Crabtree Narrowboat Hire is perfect for couples, families and groups of friends and lets you combine your boating holiday with cycling, walking, a spot of fishing or simply enjoying the passing countryside from a new angle.

Crabtree Narrowboat Hire,
Crabtree Farm, Hagg Lane,
St Michael's-On-Wyre,
Preston, Lancs. PR3 0UJ

01995 671712
07572 664949

info@crabtreenarrowboathire.com • www.crabtreenarrowboathire.com

CATTERALL • 45 – 58

The Brock Aqueduct is the largest river crossing since leaving Preston and is worth closer examination. Due to the nature of the topography, the canal builders were forced to lower the level of the river and to construct a weir on the upstream side in order to build the aqueduct of sufficient strength. At this point, there is an uninterrupted view of the Bowland Fells, Parlick and Fair Snape Fell, whilst a little further south lies the lower tree-clad summit of Beacon Fell, now a country park.

From Beacon Fell on a clear day one can view the whole of the Fylde plain and the coast. From Brock Aqueduct the canal turns east for a short distance, passing a new marina and garden centre, then after crossing under the A6 it runs close to the railway and the M6 for a couple of miles. The strange Dalek-like structure on the towpath side, just north of Bridge 48, is a borehole wellhead, many of which can be seen in the area.

On the approach to Catterall, the canal passes through a pleasant wooded stretch. The house on the left just before Bridge 51 has been converted from a former stable for the horses and attendants for the passenger boat service. Bridge 52 is the Calder Aqueduct, an inverted siphon, and just north of the basin beyond Bridge 53 a small feeder enters the canal from the River Calder. The remains of Garstang and Catterall railway station on the main line, is beside Bridge 54. This was once the junction of the branch line through Garstang and Pilling to Knott End on the coast. Both the branch line and the station closed many years ago and there is very little left to see. About 2 miles along the lane north east of Bridge 54 lies the tiny village of Calder Vale, nestling in the valley of the River Calder. The western flank of the Pennines is now visible to the east.

CATTERALL Bridges 45 – 58

Greenhalgh Castle: Built by the Earl of Derby in 1490. During The Civil War, it was held for the King and was almost the last place to hold out against the Parliamentary forces. Ruins visible between Br.57 & 58. Access is from Br.56 via a marked footpath; at the tarmac lane close to the castle go left for 150yds, through the field gate and double back along the hedge. Access is often muddy.

MARINAS/BOATHIRE

Barton Grange Marina Farm Shop & Garden Centre, Br.47. ☎️🏧📶🅾️🅿️. Tel: 01995 642900 www.bartongrange.co.uk

Narrow Boat Hire & Holidays at Barton Grange Marina. Tel: 01253 356399 / 07977 683282

Lancaster Canal Boats, at Barton Grange Marina. Waterbus service, special cruises and private charters. Tel: 01524 389410 www.budgietransport.co.uk

Water Farm Boat Hire, at Barton Grange Marina. Tel: 01524 853940 www.waterfarmboathire.co.uk

Crabtree Narrowboat Hire, at Barton Grange Marina. Tel: 01995 671712 Mob: 07572 664949 www.crabtreenarrowboathire.com

'The Margaret Kane', at Barton Grange Marina, a purpose built wheelchair-accessible wide beam boat providing short residential breaks and day trips for families who have a child with additional needs. Tel: 01253 761334 www.kensingtonfoundation.com

FOOD

SPAR shop, immediately N of Br.49. Access gate from towpath. Also garage, petrol & diesel Tel: 01995 640231.

PUBS

Brockholes Arms, Catterall. ½ mile W of Br.51. SD 502 425. Tel: 01995 640369

Kenlis Arms, Catterall. 200yd E of Br.54 Tel: 01995 603307.Tel: 01772 691866

Access to towpath
KEY
L Level Path
R Ramp
S Steps
G Gate/Chicane
sT Stile

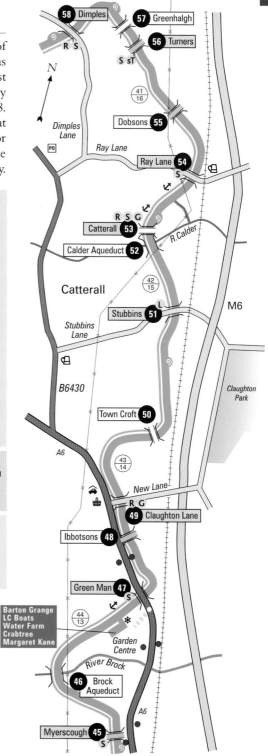

Duck Island Boat Company...

The fastest way to slow down

Garstang Marina

The fastest way to slow down... cruising in superior style aboard a luxurious bespoke wide beam canal boat or luxury narrow boat. If this is your idea of unique holiday heaven, then join us at Duck Island Boat Company and enjoy the best canal boat experience you have ever had. Situated on the beautiful **42 mile lock-free** Lancaster Canal in the heart of Lancashire, we offer an intriguing opportunity for a spot of pure relaxation and self indulgence.

We are a small family run company offering luxury wide beam canal barge & narrow boat holiday hire on one of the longest lock free stretches in the UK's inland waterway system the Lancaster Canal.

We are particularly proud that we have designed all our boats...they are all bespoke so you won't have experienced boats like ours before.

The Boats

Canal boat hire is not typically associated with luxury but then we are not a typical hire boat company. Quite simply we aim to provide the best canal boats & the highest level of service to ensure that your holiday is everything you hoped it to be & more.

Our boats are smartly painted in aubergine & cream and traditionally hand sign written – the interiors are beautifully finished with quality fixtures and fittings incorporating many features you would want on your own boat

It goes without saying that a good night's sleep is essential for a happy holiday so each boat has a fixed bed with a luxurious mattress, sumptuous duvet/pillows and hotel quality bed linen.

The bathrooms have luxury glass shower enclosures, porcelain sinks with stylish vanity units and toilets which flush at the touch of a button.

The quality contemporary kitchens are fully equipped with everything you need and cleverly designed to incorporate a full sized cooker and fridge.

Be prepared for your immaculate boat to be admired as you cruise past other holiday makers!

Duck Island Boat Company
For further details please visit our website:
www.lancastercanalboathire.com or telephone **07925 236 621**

You are now on the outskirts of Garstang but as the canal skirts round the south-west side of this small town, urbanisation does not intrude. The River Wyre is crossed on a majestic single arch aqueduct with the river thirty feet below. The aqueduct is best viewed from the footpath running along the river bank which can be accessed by the steps from the towing path. Just beyond lies Garstang basin. The building on the north side is a Tithe Barn, predating the canal by over a hundred years and built of brick, a rarely used material at that time. The building is now used as a restaurant. Many old industrial and agricultural artefacts hang from the roof and walls of the barn. From here it is a couple of minutes walk to the town centre. 7-day visitor moorings, Br.60 – 63. Moss Lane sanitary station is at Bridge 63. The pipe bridge (63a) to the north of Garstang carries water from Barnacre Reservoir to Blackpool and the Fylde. The canal passes quickly back into rural Lancashire. On the offside is Bridge House Marina which has all facilities for boaters. A little further north are the remains of Bridge 65 which carried the former 'Pilling Pig' railway, a branch line running from Garstang to Knott End at the mouth of the River Wyre. A few yards further on is the entrance to Garstang Marina with all facilities for boaters. The canal continues to wind through the countryside, hugging the 70 foot contour. The canal sides are rich with yellow flag, yellow water lily and watermint. A few miles to the east are the windswept fells of the Forest of Bowland, which rise to 1840 ft (561m) at Ward's Stone, the highest point in Lancashire.

Garstang: PO; Tel; Shops; Banks; Pubs; Tourist Information. A charming market town, one of the most important in Lancashire and mentioned in the Domesday Book. The 18th century Church of St. Thomas is near Bridge 62. The interesting Town Hall was rebuilt in 1939 to replace the original 1680 building, constructed when King Charles II conferred Borough status on the town. In 2000 Garstang became the world's first Fairtrade Town and has a good selection of shops, including supermarkets. There is a market on Thursday on the cobbled market place and up the High Street. Buses run from here to Preston, Blackpool and Lancaster.

St. Helens Church: Two miles south of Garstang. Anyone interested in churches should visit this ancient parish church, known as The Cathedral of the Fylde, and situated in an attractive setting near the River Wyre at Churchtown, a short bus ride from Garstang. The Wyre Way footpath opposite Garstang Basin leads to the church. Most of the structure is 15th century but parts are Norman in origin. The roof beams are made from four oaks that Henry IV gave to Churchtown when forests were still the property of the crown.

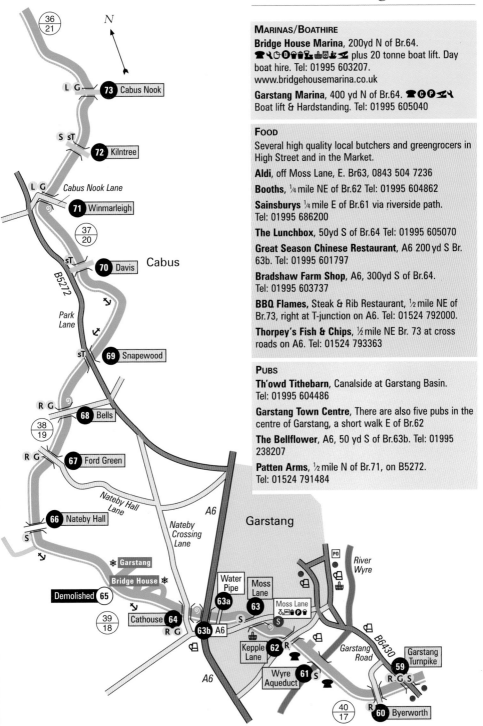

MARINAS/BOATHIRE

Bridge House Marina, 200yd N of Br.64.
🕿🖳🕒🌀🍴🚿🛢🛏🖥🛟🛒 plus 20 tonne boat lift. Day boat hire. Tel: 01995 603207.
www.bridgehousemarina.co.uk

Garstang Marina, 400 yd N of Br.64. 🕿🕒🌀🛟🏴
Boat lift & Hardstanding. Tel: 01995 605040

FOOD

Several high quality local butchers and greengrocers in High Street and in the Market.

Aldi, off Moss Lane, E. Br63, 0843 504 7236

Booths, ¼ mile NE of Br.62 Tel: 01995 604862

Sainsburys ¼ mile E of Br.61 via riverside path. Tel: 01995 686200

The Lunchbox, 50yd S of Br.64 Tel: 01995 605070

Great Season Chinese Restaurant, A6 200 yd S Br. 63b. Tel: 01995 601797

Bradshaw Farm Shop, A6, 300yd S of Br.64. Tel: 01995 603737

BBQ Flames, Steak & Rib Restaurant, ½ mile NE of Br.73, right at T-junction on A6. Tel: 01524 792000.

Thorpey's Fish & Chips, ½ mile NE Br. 73 at cross roads on A6. Tel: 01524 793363

PUBS

Th'owd Tithebarn, Canalside at Garstang Basin. Tel: 01995 604486

Garstang Town Centre, There are also five pubs in the centre of Garstang, a short walk E of Br.62

The Bellflower, A6, 50 yd S of Br.63b. Tel: 01995 238207

Patten Arms, ½ mile N of Br.71, on B5272. Tel: 01524 791484

Bridge House Marina & Caravan Park

Between bridges 68 & 69 and just off the A6 on the outskirts of Garstang.

Bridge 64

A marina with so much more...

Set in a scenic location on the banks of the Lancaster Canal, Bridge House Marina is well connected to the main systems of England. Established in 1974 our marina has a wealth of experience with personnel having a combined boating knowledge of some 50 plus years.

Boat Lifting:
- Wide Beam contact for details
- Narrowboats
- Cruisers
- In/Out of Water
- On/Off Transport

Cruisers:
- Powerwashing
- Antifouling
- Storage Inside/out including power & water supply

Narrowboats:
- Powerwashing
- Blacking
- Anodes – Supply & Fitting
- Storage
- Hard Standing or Polytunnel Both include power & water supply

Slipway:
- The Marina has a slipway for slipping boats in/out.

Other on-site facilities:
- On Site Chandlery Superstore
- The Boat & Outboard Centre
- Marine Engineer
- Marine Heating Engineer
- Boat Safety Examiner
- Boat Builder

The Site also offers:
- Day Boat Hire
- Caravan/Motorhome Touring Park

Bridge House Marina is a Canal & River Trust Agent providing
- LICENCES – short/long term
- PUMP OUT CARDS
- SERVICE STATION KEYS
- ANTI VANDAL KEYS

New and Used Boat Sales and Brokerage

We at BHM have been Marine Brokers since 1974 dealing in both steel Narrow boats and GRP cruisers. Being a family firm we are able to provide a personal and friendly service. We offer all the facilities you would expect from a modern broker, part exchange and for those who wish it, we also purchase craft (subject to conditions). Please feel free to contact our sales office whether you wish to purchase a craft or sell your own.

Bridgehouse Marina & Caravan Park, Nateby Crossing Lane, Nateby, Nr Garstang, PR3 0JJ

Email: info@bridgehousemarina.co.uk
www.bridgehousemarina.co.uk

A tranquil picturesque setting midway on the Lancaster Canal

Bridge 64

Garstang Marina offers a variety of facilities along with a warm friendly welcome

FACILITIES INCLUDE:
- Moorings with electric points
- Showers, Toilets, Sluice, Laundry
- Calor gas, Diesel and Coal
- Temporary moorings
- Boat Lifting/Storage
- Car Parking

The Marina now accommodates over 270 moorings, for boats up to 70' – steel and GRP cruisers. The Marina is uniquely set in a sheltered landscaped valley within walking distance of Garstang's Historic Market Town which was voted best Town for its floral displays. It also offers a variety of shops, café, restaurants and local pubs.

Boat Lifting Service for Cruisers, Steel Boats and Wide Beams • Lifting • Powerwashing • Workshop • Hardstanding Storage inside/outside

We look forward to seeing you soon

www.garstangmarina.co.uk Email – enquiries@garstangmarina.co.uk
Garstang Marina, Nateby Crossing Lane, Garstang PR3 0JJ Tel: 01995 605040

FORTON • 74 – 85

Just prior to Ratcliffe Bridge (75) on the offside is Ratcliffe Wharf. This was once busy with canal barges and is now a long term mooring with a water point. The mounds behind the mooring are old lime kilns, which were common along the length of the canal. Barges would bring in limestone and coal, and the lime was burnt. The burnt 'Quicklime' was used to improve farmland and to make mortar. North of Bridge 75 is a particularly attractive stretch of the canal. Notice the number of small canalside woodlands. Most were originally planted with larch to provide timber for canal related works. Some larch remain; they are characterised by their swooping branches and curved needles. Forton lies a mile south-east of Bridge 79. It was for a time the richest village in England due to the payments received when the M6 motorway was built. The small basin at Richmond Bridge was constructed for transhipment of stone from

the nearby quarry, now disused. At Bridge 84 is Ellel Grange, built between 1857 and 1859. The bridge is more ornate in style, in keeping with the secluded mansion. The next bridge along (85) is Double Bridge. The bridge was to lie at the boundary between two farms, so the Canal Company had to build a 'double' bridge with a dividing wall down the centre. North of Double Bridge is an impressive cutting in solid rock.

FORTON **Bridges 74 – 85**

MARINAS/BOATHIRE
Water Babies Narrowboat Hire, based at Br.78.
Tel: 0745 3366221 www.water-babies.co.uk

FOOD
SPAR, ½ mile NE of Br.73, or ¾ mile SE of Br.75, on
A6. General store. Also garage, petrol, diesel & gas.
Tel: 01524 791470
Wallings Farm, on B5272 – 1 mile NW of Br.75. Local
foods. Tel: 01524 791100. Coffee shop, restaurant, ice
cream parlour. Tel: 01524 793781
Old Holly Farm, ½ mile NE of Br. 73 by road, or ½ mile
E of Br.74 by footpath. Farm shop, tea room, animals,
children's activities. Tel: 01524 791200

PUBS
New Holly, Forton, ¾ mile E of Br.75 on A6 (bear left
at T-junction). Tel: 01524 793500
Bay Horse, ½ mile E of Br.81. First left and across A6.
Tel: 01524 791204

Access to towpath
KEY
L Level Path
R Ramp
S Steps
G Gate/Chicane
sT Stile

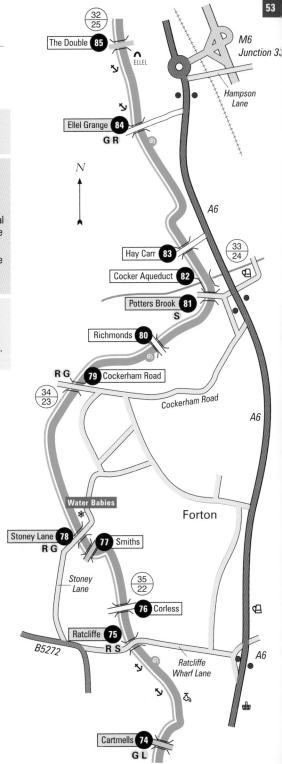

water babies
narrow boat hire

On the beautiful Lancaster Canal

Water Babies was one of the first narrow boat hire companies on the canal. We are a small family-run narrowboat hire company, we pride ourselves on offering a friendly and flexible service with a personal touch.

The Lancaster Canal offers 42 miles of lock-free cruising – stunning views – Historic cities – The Lune aqueduct – picturesque market towns – excellent Pubs and Eateries along the route. If a canal holiday is new to you, please be assured that full instructions and demonstration on how to handle and operate every aspect of the boat will be given by a fully qualified RYA Inland Waterways Helmsman Instructor – the only one on the length of the canal!. When you feel comfortable and confident the Skipper's hat will be yours!

Simply give Paul a call on:
07453 366 221 or 07813 014 089
or visit: www.water-babies.co.uk/

GLASSON BRANCH

The junction with the Glasson Branch is marked by the lock keeper's cottage and a graceful bridge carrying the main line towpath over the branch. The branch was opened in 1826 and it provided a vital link to the sea. There are six locks to Glasson Basin, with another down to Glasson Dock. The top gates of the locks are padlocked for security reasons (standard Canal & River Trust key). The lock gates should be shut after use and the lock should be left empty, even when ascending. The flight gently descends to the sea, following the line of the River Conder which runs into the River Lune at Glasson. There are good views around, especially to the slopes of Clougha Pike. Close to Lock 4 is Thurnham Hall, which is now a timeshare complex, with its chapel and woodlands. Beside Lock 6 is The Mill at Conder Green. The mill was at one time fed by canal water from above Lock 5 – part of the old mill race can still be seen next to the towpath – the tail race returning the water to the canal below Lock 6. The canal company purchased the mill in 1824 for £1,100 in order to obtain its right to take water from the River Conder and divert it via the canal to the mill wheel. The old mill has been restored and is now a hotel and restaurant. The canal ends at the Basin where there is a large boatyard and 9-day visitor moorings.

Glasson Dock was opened in 1787 as part of the Port of Lancaster. Grain and timber were the main imports and coal to Ireland was the main export. The canal branch, completed in 1826, leads into Glasson Basin which in turn locks through into Glasson Dock. The basin covers twelve acres, serving as a reservoir for the outer dock at low tides. It could accommodate vessels up to 200 tons, and at one time small sea-going vessels sailed up the canal to Kendal and Preston. The opening of Preston Dock in 1892 brought Glasson's period of greatness to an end, though nowadays it is still busy with exports of bulk cargoes to the Isle of Man and the Western Isles of Scotland, and the import of fertiliser and animal foodstuffs.

Glasson: PO (Mon & Thursday only); Tel; Stores; Café. Glasson Village is built round the dock and basin and from here there are delightful walks near the Lune Estuary; Cockersand Abbey 2 miles to the south and the 4 mile footpath & cycle path along the disused railway line to Lancaster are both recommended. Sea-going craft can go through the dock and sea lock out into the Lune Estuary, and thence to the Irish Sea. It is also possible to travel up the River Lune to Lancaster if the tide conditions are right, although this is not recommended for most canal craft. To use the lock between the Basin and the Dock you should contact C&RT (see p.92), at least 24hrs beforehand.

Thurnham Hall: ½ mile S of Br.6. A battlemented 16th century Mansion, once the family home of the Daltons.

GLASSON BRANCH

MARINAS/BOATHIRE

BWML Glasson Basin Marina, Road access in School Lane 200yd W of Br.8.
Shop Tues–Sat 9am–4.30pm, Workshop Mon–Friday.
⚓🛒🔧🅿⛽🚿🛠🚾▣(tokens). Tel: 01524 751491.
www.bwml.co.uk

FOOD

Port of Lancaster Smokehouse, W of the dock, 250yd from basin. Smoked fish, meats, cheeses and other fine foods. Tel: 01524 751493
Lantern o'er Lune Café adjacent to Br.9 (swing bridge) 01524 753323

PUBS

Dalton Arms, W of the dock, 200yd from basin.
Tel: 01524 753007

Stork, Conder Green. ¼ mile N of Br.6.
Tel: 01524 751234

The Mill at Conder Green, by Lock 6,
Tel. 01524 752852

Access to towpath
KEY
L Level Path
R Ramp
S Steps
G Gate/Chicane
sT Stile

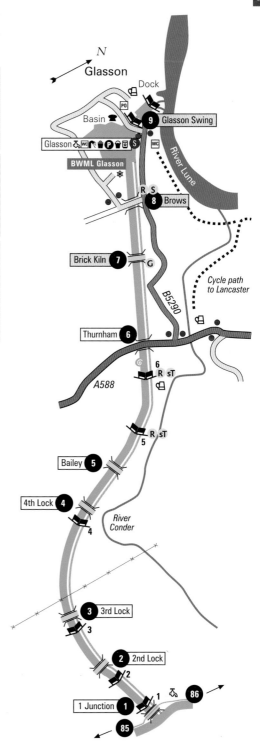

Half a mile north of Glasson Junction is the small village of Galgate. The canal skirts around Galgate and after passing over the River Conder Aqueduct, enters rather flat country until it reaches Brant Beck Bridge (91) where it enters Burrow Heights Cutting, more familiarly known as Deep Cutting. This was built through glacial deposits in order to avoid a long detour. The cutting is up to 30 feet deep and well over a mile long: the largest cutting on this canal. Its wooded slopes are a haven for wildlife, possibly the best area on the canal to see kingfishers. The gateway to the southern end of the cutting is majestic. Between Bridges 91 & 92 an inverted siphon carries Burrow Beck beneath the canal and can be seen from the towpath. The northern end of Deep Cutting is marked by a view to Lancaster Castle. Bargees know this as 'Hangman's Corner' – apparently condemned prisoners being exercised here gave it that name.

Galgate: PO; Tel; Stores. A busy village dominated by the railway which passes through on a tall viaduct. A useful place to stop for provisions or refreshment. It also has a handy Fish and Chip shop. The Mill on the east of the town was the oldest silk mill in England and has now been converted to industrial units. From Galgate there is a good footpath, partly along the canal, to Glasson Dock 2 miles to the west. 7-day visitor moorings Br.85 – 86 with a water point. Sanitary station at Galgate Marina. (See Note on p19 & p61.)

GALGATE **Bridges 86 – 93**

MARINAS/BOATHIRE
BWML Galgate Marina, Br.86.
🅿*, ♿🍴🛒(tokens). Tel: 01524 751491.
www.bwml.co.uk

Note: *Prepay cards and tokens for BWML Galgate can only be purchased at Galgate & Glasson. Galgate is only staffed Tues 10am–12.30pm, Fri–Sun

10am–3pm
FOOD
SPAR shop, Main Road, Galgate. ¼ mile N of Br.86.

PUBS
Plough Inn, Galgate. 50yd N of Br.86.
Tel: 01524 751337

New Inn, Galgate. ¼ mile N of Br.86.
Tel: 01524 752932

CAFÉ
Canalside Craft Centre, Galgate. Own mooring at Br.86. Café, crafts, books. Tel: 01524 752223

Access to towpath
KEY
- **L** Level Path
- **R** Ramp
- **S** Steps
- **G** Gate/Chicane
- **sT** Stile

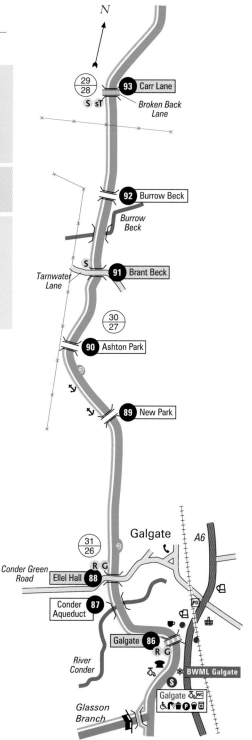

63

Bridge 98A

lancaster's award-winning canalside pub

- large selection of real ales • selection of fine wines • extensive, locally sourced menu •
- warm and friendly welcome •
- cheese & deli boards •

thewaterwitch

canal tow path
aldcliffe lane
lancaster
la1 1su

book a table
(01524) 63828

visit our website
www.waterwitchlancaster.co.uk

say hello...
thewaterwitch@mitchellspubs.co.uk

follow us on facebook and twitter to keep up to date with our latest news and offers ...

Bridge 100

THE WHITE CROSS
CASK ALE PUB & RESTAURANT

EXCELLENT FOOD
ALL DAY, EVERY DAY
12PM - 9PM

LANCASTER'S LARGEST
SELECTION OF CASK ALE
14 REAL HAND PUMPS, PLUS 2 CRAFT PUMPS

MOORING SPACES RIGHT
OUTSIDE THE PUB
ONLY 5 MINS WALK FROM CITY CENTER

WWW.THEWHITECROSS.CO.UK   01524 33999

Passing under the main line railway, Bridge 97, one soon arrives at the old packet-boat house and adjoining wharf on the right. This was used for repairing packet or passenger boats between 1833 and 1843. The building held two boats with workshops above. It contained a hoist by which boats could be lifted to the upper floors. Note that the front is skewed – this allowed the launching of these long thin boats. The building was saved from dereliction and restored in the 1990s, and is now converted into apartments as part of a housing development on the former British Waterways yard.

Opposite is the 'Aldcliffe Triangle', a small, once derelict plot previously used by a paving contractor and a boat-builder. It has been successfully reclaimed and developed by a local community group. Alongside is one of the three turnover bridges on the canal (98). These allowed the horse towing the barge to change sides of the canal without unhitching. Years of wear by the tow ropes has resulted in an iron bridge plate on the towing path side being badly worn. Close by Bridge 98 is a chip shop and laundrette. Beyond Bridge 98 are two large canal basins and the Waterwitch public house, which used to be canal stables. The basins were originally covered and were used for the loading/unloading of barges; the

MARINAS/BOATHIRE

Lancaster Canal Boats, Br.99. Water bus service, special cruises and private charters. Tel: 01524 389410 www.budgietransport.co.uk

FOOD

Shops & Supermarket in Lancaster city centre, street market Wednesday & Saturday, Sainsburys Local and Tesco Express 100yds N Br.99

Quay Chip Shop at Br.98. Tel: 01524 62487

Petrol & diesel garage & general store 50yds W of Br.105.

SPAR shop Slyne Road, at Br.110. Tel: 01524 530050

PUBS

There are numerous pubs in the centre of Lancaster, best reached from Bridge 99. There is also a good selection of shops, restaurants and the usual fast food establishments.

Waterwitch, Br.98a canalside. Housed in former packet boat stables. Tel: 01524 63828

Toll House Inn, at Br.99. Tel: 01524 599900

White Cross, Br.100 canalside. Tel: 01524 33999

Golden Lion, Moor Lane, Lancaster, Br.102 Tel: 01524 84219

adjacent wharves now have student accommodation. This is the best area to moor up and explore the city of Lancaster. 7-day visitor moorings & sanitary station. Many of the former canalside mills have been put to new use as offices and housing. Bridge 100 brings the towpath back to the west side once again after less than half a mile on the east side. Mooring rings and canalside seats are available between Bridges 100 and 102. At Bridge 101 is the RC Cathedral of St Peter, while the Anglican Priory and the Castle can be seen across the City centre from the canal between Bridges 102 and 103. The canal winds north from Lancaster then suddenly turns left across Bulk Aqueduct over the main road to the M6. Rennie's original narrow stone structure was replaced by a modern concrete trough in 1961 to allow road widening. A rail mounted cradle conveyed boats across a temporary bridge during construction. The canal continues along a huge embankment to the Lune Aqueduct and around the northern outskirts of Lancaster.

LANCASTER **Bridges 94 – 110**

ATTRACTIONS

Maritime Museum, St. George's Quay. Includes canal history and a full-size replica of the packet boat 'Waterwitch'. Admission charge. Open daily. Tel: 01524 382264

Lancaster City Museum and King's Own Royal Regiment Museum, Market Square. Prehistoric, Roman and Mediaeval exhibits; history of the Regiment. Free admission. Closed Mondays. Tel: 01524 64637

Judges Lodgings, Judges Lodgings, Church Street. Built in 1675 (currently closed).

Cottage Museum, 15, Castle Hill. Life was in the 18th century. Admission charge. Open Easter to September, afternoons. Tel: 01524 64637

Lancaster Castle, Tours start every ½ hour. Admission charge. Open daily Tel: 01524 64998

Priory Church, Castle Hill. Built between 1380 and 1430. Open daily.

St Peter's Cathedral, St Peter's Road, Br 100/101. 1859 a superb example of architect E.G. Paley's work.

Williamson Park, Quernemore Road ½ mile E of Br.102. Café, woodland, ornamental lake, Butterfly (Palm) House mini beasts & birds, Ashton Memorial Edwardian folly.

Gregson Arts and Community Centre, 200yd E of Br.102. Bar, food, arts & events. Tel: 01524 849959

THEATRE AND CINEMA:

The Dukes, Moor Lane 250yd W of Br 102. Films and live theatre. Tel: 01524 598500

Lancaster Grand Theatre, St Leonard's Gate, 300yd NW of Br 102. Home to Lancaster Footlights and a wide range of local and visiting productions. Tel: 01524 64695

Vue multi screen cinema, Church Street / Market Square. Tel: 0871 224 0240

Access to towpath
KEY
L Level Path
R Ramp
S Steps
G Gate/Chicane
sT Stile

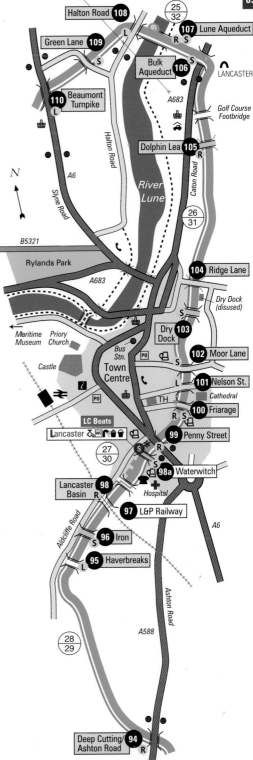

Lune Aqueduct: The aqueduct was formally opened on 22nd November 1797. It took five years to build and cost £48,000. It stands on wooden piles driven twenty feet into the river bed; its 5 semi-circular arches each spanning 70 feet. The canal is 51 feet above the river and the whole structure is 664 feet (202m) long. Designed by John Rennie and built from local sandstone, it is considered to be one of the most beautiful aqueducts in the country and is a Grade 1 listed structure. It is certainly the finest piece of engineering on the Lancaster Canal. Take the steps or ramp from the towpath down to the south bank of the river (or the steps on the north side) for the best appreciation of the grandeur of the structure. Waterbus stop at N end of the aqueduct. A £2.4m project was carried out between January 2011 – March 2012 to restore the Aqueduct including repairs to the channel, masonry, removal of graffiti and vegetation plus improvements to public/disabled access.

Lancaster: This historic city, once the busiest seaport on the West coast, still retains much of its character. It was originally the site of a Roman fortress and a crossing of the

Preston, Blackpool and Kendal. Trains to all major destinations (see p.89).

Lancaster Castle: An impressive fortress, built mainly in the 13th and 14th centuries, set on the heights overlooking the city. It has a Norman Keep and a beacon tower known as John of Gaunt's seat. A drawing of the John O'Gaunt gateway was used by the original Lancaster Canal Company for its seal and a carved relief of it adorns the keystone of the centre span of the Lune Aqueduct. The Shire Hall has an extensive collection of heraldic shields. The castle now houses a crown court. The famous Pendle witches were tried here. It is open for tours daily, except when the courts are in session. Check opening times on 01524 64998.

Lancaster was designated a Cycling Demonstration Town in 2005, one of six English towns to receive extra funding to improve cycling facilities and increase cycle use. This has resulted in many improvements to the cycle route network, including the canal

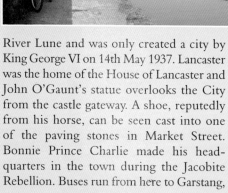

River Lune and was only created a city by King George VI on 14th May 1937. Lancaster was the home of the House of Lancaster and John O'Gaunt's statue overlooks the City from the castle gateway. A shoe, reputedly from his horse, can be seen cast into one of the paving stones in Market Street. Bonnie Prince Charlie made his headquarters in the town during the Jacobite Rebellion. Buses run from here to Garstang,

towpath. Cyclists may now join the towpath at numerous points between Bridges 94 & 129. The Lancaster and Morecambe Greenway is a traffic-free shared use path running from Lancaster's striking Millennium Bridge through to Morecambe's Promenade. The Prom cycle route has connections south to Heysham and north to Hest Bank and Carnforth, including a link to the canal towpath at Rushley Drive just south of Br 117.

River Lune Millennium Park

A former railway line linking Glasson Dock to Lancaster and the Lune Valley forms the route of the River Lune Millennium Park. A 9-mile shared use path runs along the south and east bank of the river from Glasson Dock, via St George's Quay, and eastwards to Bull Beck, just east of Caton. This is well worth a detour away from the canal, on foot or by bike. A ramp and a flight of steps just south of the aqueduct joins the canal towpath to the riverside path.

Passing under the aqueduct, the remnants of industry that developed with the coming of the railway are evident but this ends as you initially pass beneath the new bridge linking the M6 to Heysham (opened in 2016) and then the impressive single parabolic arched span of the motorway bridge. A little further on, the remains of Halton station are connected to the village on the opposite bank of the river by an iron bridge. After Halton the valley narrows into a deep wooded gorge: the river

running deep past the remains of former mills on the opposite bank, now redeveloped with many new houses. Had Brindley's original survey been followed, the canal would have crossed the river at this point.

The Crook O'Lune is a delightful spot where the river makes a horseshoe loop and the path crosses the river twice within a few hundred yards. Turner certainly appreciated the beauty here since he painted the scene from the viewpoint at Gray's Seat, reached by a short detour. The area has been designated a country park; car parking, café, toilets and information panels are provided for the visitor. The walker may choose to return to the canal by following a series of footpaths on the north bank of the river, although this route involves some road walking. The Millennium Park features public works of art and interpretive panels along its length. A descriptive leaflet is available from the Lancaster Visitor Information Centre. Those whose legs give up will be pleased to know that buses run through Caton into Lancaster, passing beneath the canal at Bulk Aqueduct (106).

Morecambe: A short train, bus or cycle ride from Lancaster. The seafront has the spectacular backdrop of Morecambe Bay and a statue of Morecambe's famous son, Eric.

Heysham Village: This has a quaint main street and is famous for the ruins of St. Patrick's Chapel and the Viking rock graves, as well as its Nettle Beer. The Port of Heysham has several cargo ferry routes to Ireland and passenger, car and freight services to the Isle of Man.

HEST BANK • 111 – 125

The canal runs northwards into pleasant countryside with views across Morecambe Bay and the hills of the Lake District. The new Milestone Bridge (Br.111a) carries the newly constructed M6 to Heysham link road (Bay Gateway) opened in 2016, over the canal adjacent to the milestone 3m from Lancaster, 24 miles to Kendal. At Hest Bank, the canal runs very near to the shore and, before the Glasson Branch was built in 1826, goods were trans-shipped here between sailing boats in Morecambe Bay and canal barges. The Hest Bank Hotel lay on the coaching route to Grange-over-Sands on the opposite side of the Bay. A light in the window facing the shore would guide coachmen across the sands. After Hest Bank, the canal continues close to the sea passing through Bolton-le-Sands. The Packet Boat Inn (now closed) was one of the stopping points for passenger 'packet' boats. There would have been a landing stage on the offside and steps up to the inn. From 1833 a fast passenger service operated, completing the journey between Preston and Kendal in less than eight hours; by far the swiftest and most comfortable mode of transport at the time. The service was withdrawn in 1846 when the Lancaster and Carlisle Railway was opened. Adjacent to Bridge 115 is the site of a ruined packet boat stables.

Hest Bank: Telephone, Stores and Waterbus stop. Once busy with canal boats and inland vessels, this is now a suburb of Lancaster and Morecambe. It is the nearest the canal comes to the sea, which is only a few hundred yards away at high water. The sands are uncovered at low water and in summer there are guided walks six miles across the Bay to Kents Bank. Details of guided walks available at the café on the foreshore. On no account should visitors venture across the sands without a guide. There are opportunities here for bird watching (refer to RSPB, Tel: 01524 701601). 14-day visitor moorings, Br.116 – 117.

Bolton-le-Sands: PO; Tel; Stores, Waterbus stop. An attractive village which takes pride in its canal, with many gardens landscaped down to the water. 14-day visitor moorings, Br.124 – 125.

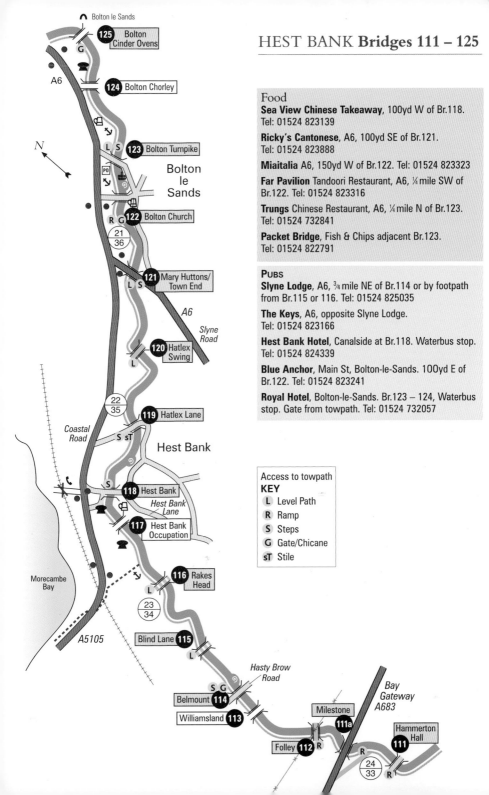

Map Labels

- Bolton le Sands
- **125** Bolton Cinder Ovens
- G
- A6
- **124** Bolton Chorley
- **123** Bolton Turnpike — L S
- Bolton le Sands
- PO
- R G **122** Bolton Church
- 21 / 36
- **121** Mary Huttons/ Town End — L S
- A6
- Slyne Road
- **120** Hatlex Swing — L
- 22 / 35
- **119** Hatlex Lane
- Coastal Road — S sT
- Hest Bank
- S — **118** Hest Bank
- Hest Bank Lane
- **117** Hest Bank Occupation
- Morecambe Bay
- **116** Rakes Head — L
- 23 / 34
- A5105
- Blind Lane **115** — L
- Hasty Brow Road
- S G — Belmount **114**
- Williamsland **113**
- Milestone
- Bay Gateway A683
- **111a**
- Hammerton Hall
- Folley **112** R
- **111**
- 24 / 33 — R
- N

Food

Sea View Chinese Takeaway, 100yd W of Br.118.
Tel: 01524 823139

Ricky's Cantonese, A6, 100yd SE of Br.121.
Tel: 01524 823888

Miaitalia A6, 150yd W of Br.122. Tel: 01524 823323

Far Pavilion Tandoori Restaurant, A6, ¼ mile SW of Br.122. Tel: 01524 823316

Trungs Chinese Restaurant, A6, ¼ mile N of Br.123.
Tel: 01524 732841

Packet Bridge, Fish & Chips adjacent Br.123.
Tel: 01524 822791

PUBS

Slyne Lodge, A6, ¾ mile NE of Br.114 or by footpath from Br.115 or 116. Tel: 01524 825035

The Keys, A6, opposite Slyne Lodge.
Tel: 01524 823166

Hest Bank Hotel, Canalside at Br.118. Waterbus stop.
Tel: 01524 824339

Blue Anchor, Main St, Bolton-le-Sands. 100yd E of Br.122. Tel: 01524 823241

Royal Hotel, Bolton-le-Sands. Br.123 – 124, Waterbus stop. Gate from towpath. Tel: 01524 732057

Access to towpath
KEY

- **L** Level Path
- **R** Ramp
- **S** Steps
- **G** Gate/Chicane
- **sT** Stile

CARNFORTH • 126 – 130

Between Bolton-le-Sands and Tewitfield the canal provides excellent views across Morecambe Bay to the Lakeland mountains. Close to Thwaite End Bridge (127) there is access to bus services to Lancaster, Kendal, Kellets etc. Entering Carnforth, the canal widens and there are 7-day visitor moorings and sanitary station on the left and Nu-Way Acorn Marina on the right. There is a garage and convenience shop with access from the towpath and a large supermarket just across the A6. After Carnforth the canal crosses under the M6 at junction 35 and heads out into open country once more, passing less than a mile NW of the award winning village of Over Kellet. On the offside at Bridge 130 there is an old stone wharf with road access.

Carnforth: PO; Stores; Garage; Tel; Banks; Station; Waterbus stop. Carnforth grew from a small village with the coming of first the canal and then the railway. Trains leave here for Barrow/Ravenglass (for Eskdale)/Sellafield, for Lancaster/Preston/Manchester Airport and for the Skipton/Leeds line. The station visitor centre includes the Brief Encounter refreshment room exhibition and gift shop. There are bus services to nearby places of interest.

Pine Lake Resort: A mile north of Carnforth on the A6/M6 jcn. Watersports. There is a footpath from Capernwray Bridge (131) following the River Keer to Pine Lake. Tel: 01524 736190.

Warton Village and Warton Crag: A mile and a half north of Carnforth. St. Oswald's Church dates back to the 13th century. The ruins of the old 14th century Manor House can be seen. Strong connections with the 'Washington' family are reflected throughout the village. Warton Crag, the site of an Ironage Settlement, affords a marvellous view of Morecambe Bay.

CARNFORTH **Bridges 126 – 130**

MARINAS/BOATHIRE
Nu-Way Acorn, Carnforth. ⚓🜨➊⚓£ winter storage. Tel: 01524 734457

FOOD
Fish & Chips; Stanley Street & North Road. Off A6 just N of Canal Turn. Access from towpath to Stanley St. (via steps to Towpath Walk) or to North Road.

Peking Chinese Takeaway 32 Market St, Carnforth
Tel: 01524 736686

Tesco, A6 at Canal Turn. Tel: 03456 779837

Booths, A6 & Market St, 300yd NW of Br 128.
Tel: 01524 736680

Aldi, A6 adjacent to Booths Tel: 0800 042 0800

PUBS
County Hotel, Lancaster Rd, 200yd W of Br.128.
Tel: 01524 732469

Carnforth Hotel, Market St, 200yd W of Br.128.
Tel: 01524 732902

Royal Station Hotel, ¼ mile W of Br.128.
Tel: 01524 733636

Snug Micropub Carnforth Station. opening times vary

Canal Turn, A6, Carnforth, on towpath, adjacent to filling station. Waterbus stop. Tel: 01524 734750.

Shovel Inn, Kellet Road. 50yd W of Br.128
Tel: 01524 733402

Taps on the Green (Cross Keys) Kellet Road, 100yd E of Br.128. Tel: 01524 732749

Eagles Head, Over Kellet, ¾ mile S of Br.130.

Tel: 01524 732457
ATTRACTIONS
Carnforth Station Heritage Centre & Brief Encounter Refreshment Room, ¼ mile W Br.128 Open daily 10am to 4pm.
Tel: 01524 735165

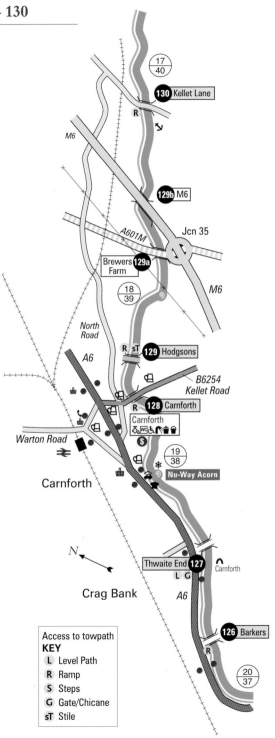

17/40

130 Kellet Lane

R

M6

129b M6

A601M

Jcn 35

Brewers **129a**
Farm

18/39

M6

North Road

A6

R sT **129** Hodgsons

B6254
Kellet Road

128 Carnforth

Carnforth

S

19/38

Nu-Way Acorn

Warton Road

Carnforth

N

Thwaite End **127**
L G
Carnforth

Crag Bank

A6

126 Barkers

R

20/37

Access to towpath
KEY
L Level Path
R Ramp
S Steps
G Gate/Chicane
sT Stile

Just north of Capernwray Bridge is the Keer Aqueduct (Br.132). Like that of the Lune, this was designed by John Rennie. It has a span of 43 feet and carries the canal 35 feet above the River Keer. Beyond is Capernwray Canal Arm, known locally as Lover's Creek. This took barges into the heart of Wegber Quarry, where they were loaded with limestone. A narrow gauge railway ran around the site, which had quarry workers houses nearby at 'New England'. The remains of the loading cranes can be seen close to the caravan site. 14-day visitor moorings near Br.134, where the canal passes Borwick Hall, an Elizabethan manor house built around a defensive Pele tower. Charles II stayed here in 1651 when his army camped in a nearby field. Bridge 138 is the last bridge on the cruising length and just beyond is the Tewitfield terminus with a picnic site, marina, 14-day visitor moorings, turning for full length boats, sanitary station, and hotel. The canal ended here prior to the section to Kendal opening in 1819 and more recently, with the building of the M6 in 1968, it again became the terminus.

So the journey by boat ends here for the time being. However, the towpath continues and is well worth exploring on foot; a mile to see the eight locks, eight miles to Stainton and the end of the canal in water, a little further to see Hincaster Tunnel or the whole 14 miles to Kendal. See the panel beside the canal for information on how the canal can be restored. Read on to find out what delights these Northern Reaches hold in store and see 'The Future for The Lancaster Canal', (page 16) for information about the Restoration project.

Tewitfield Locks: The 8 locks lift the canal 75 feet over a distance of three-quarters of a mile. These are the only locks on the 57 mile main line and were opened when the canal was extended to Kendal in 1819, 22 years after the Preston to Tewitfield section was opened. The locks were officially closed in 1968 when the M6 was constructed, but had already been disused for several years.

Leighton Hall: A mile and a half west of Tewitfield Lock 5 by public footpath to Yealand Conyers or by bus from Carnforth. A Georgian Mansion containing furniture made by R. Gillow of Lancaster, surrounded by attractive grounds. It also houses the Birds of Prey Conservation Centre. There are displays of flying eagles daily at 15:30 in fine weather. Open May to September. Tel: 01524 734474.

Leighton Moss: 3 miles west of Tewitfield Locks. RSPB nature reserve of reed marshes and large meres. It is the breeding ground of reed warblers and bitterns, but kestrels and shovellers can also be observed from the hides. Open 9.30am to 5pm (4.30 Dec & Jan) Tel. 01524 701601. Entrance charge for non-members, free if travelling by bike.

Silverdale and Arnside: 3 miles north-west of Carnforth. Area of Outstanding Natural Beauty with many public walks. Details from the Lancaster Visitor Information Centre. 01524 582394.

TEWITFIELD **Bridges 131 – 141**

MARINAS/BOATHIRE
Tewitfield Marina, Br.138 – 139. ☎.
Tel: 01524 782092 www.tewitfieldmarina.co.uk
Bluebell Narrow Boat Holidays, Tewitfield Marina,
Tel: 07854 596989
Blossom Time Narrow Boat, Tewitfield Marina,
Tel: 07984 368176 blossomtimeuk@gmail.com

PUBS
Longlands Hotel, 50yd E of canal terminus.
Tel. 01524 781256.

ATTRACTIONS
Greenlands Farm Village, 100yd E of canal terminus.
Farm shop, tea room, animals, children's activities.
Tel: 01524 784184

Commemorative Plaque

When you arrive at Tewitfield, the Lancaster
Canal Trust will be pleased to have your
comments in the form of a questionnaire which
can be downloaded from the Trust's website,
www.lctrust.co.uk. If you have arrived by boat,
you can purchase a commemorative brass
plaque by sending your details, a photo of your
boat at Tewitfield and a cheque for £8.50
(payable to LCT) along with your
questionnaire, to:
Lancaster Canal Trust,
c/o Lancaster District CVS,
The Cornerstone, Sulyard
Street, Lancaster LA1 1PX.

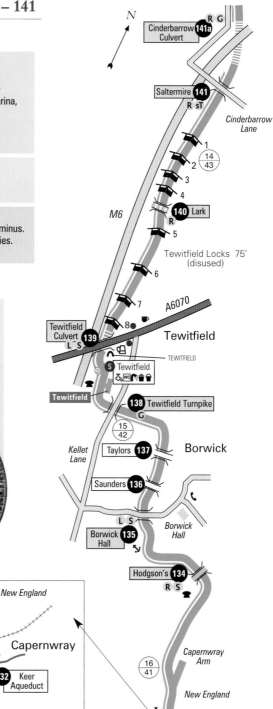

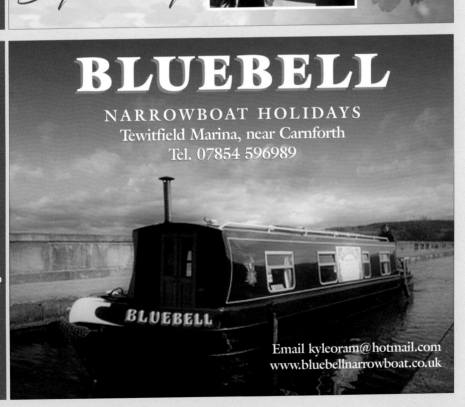

HOLME • 142 – 153

The isolated and un-navigable sections of the canal north of Tewitfield are referred to as the Northern Reaches. The canal is still in water for a further 8 miles to Stainton, acting as a water supply channel to the navigable length. The channel is often weedy but with an adequate depth of water for canoes or small craft; portages are necessary round several blockages along the canal. Walkers, however, can still follow the canal all the way to Kendal, which is very worthwhile. The towpath is a public right of way from now on and is excellent where the original canal still exists, and can easily be followed along those stretches that have been infilled. Finger posts have been provided by Lancaster Canal Trust to guide you round several major road crossings. Once away from the noise of the motorway, the canal traverses peaceful countryside, with excellent views of the Lakeland fells

and a good variety of flora and fauna. A bus service runs from Tewitfield to Kendal, passing through several of the villages along the route (Service 555; approx hourly). ¼ mile east of Bridge 142 Yealand Road, Lancaster & Morecambe Model Engineering Society operate a miniature railway at Cinderbarrow from 10.30am to 4pm on Sundays and Bank Holidays, from Easter to end of September. Tel: 01995 606767

Leaving Cinderbarrow the canal passes through quiet countryside, although one never quite loses the roar from the motorway and the nearby railway occasionally makes its presence known. After Bridge 143 an attractive wildlife information plaque produced by Burton Morewood School stands on the towpath near to the County boundary, where we pass from Lancashire into Cumbria. The old wharf that once served the village of Burton-in-Kendal is on the right. Bridge 146 is worth a closer look; it has recesses for stop gates which formerly would have been used to isolate a section of canal for maintenance purposes and to control the loss of water by leakage – a serious problem in this area of very porous limestone. Along here there are examples of the stone mileposts marking the distances between Kendal and Lancaster. Just north of Bridge 146 the milepost is on the offside. North of Holme the canal is culverted under North Road, ending an intact three and a half mile stretch from Cinderbarrow.

Northern Reaches Fragmented Sections

People often ask, "Can I use my boat on the Northern Reaches?" The answer is "yes, but…"

The table shows the status of the 6 separate sections which are still in water.

All craft require a Canal & River Trust licence to use the canal.

Between Bridges No.	Location	Length approx.	Status	Access into the water
139 – 141a	Tewitfield locks	1 mile	Not navigable	No access
141a – 153a	Burton & Holme	3 miles	Navigable for unpowered craft only	Cinderbarrow, N of Br.141a
153a – 154a	Garths Br.	½ mile	Not navigable	No access
154a – 162	Farleton	1¼ miles	Navigable for unpowered craft only	No easy access
162 – 163a	A65	½ mile	Not navigable	No access
163a – 172	Millness to Stainton	2½ miles	Navigable for trailable craft	Millness Slipway N of Br.163a

HOLME **Bridges 142 – 153**

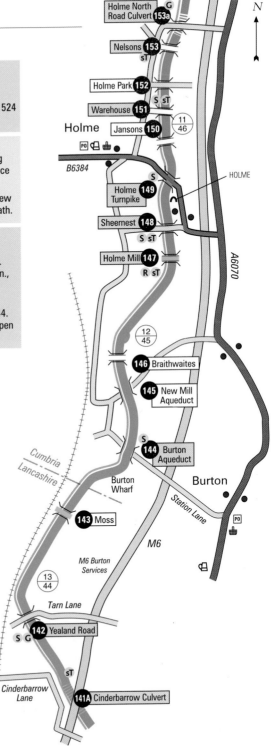

PUBS

Kings Arms, Burton, ½ mile SE of Br.144.
Tel: 01524 781409

The Smithy Inn, Holme. ¼ mile W of Br.149. Tel: 01524 781302

FOOD

Burton-in-Kendal: PO; Tel; Stores. Large interesting village ½ mile east of Burton Aqueduct (Br.144), once a staging post on the main road to the north.

Holme: PO; Tel; Stores. An old limestone village. New houses built along the canal have tended the towpath.

ATTRACTIONS

Heron Corn Mill: Beetham, on A6, 2 miles W of Holme via the Limestone Link footpath from Br.151. Historic restored C18th watermill. Open Wed. – Sun., 11am – 4pm. Also Bank Holidays. SD 497798 Tel: 015395 64271

Lakeland Wildlife Oasis: on A6, 1 mile W of Br.144. SD 509777 The North West's favourite little zoo. Open daily 10am to dusk Tel: 01539 563027.

Access to towpath
KEY
- **L** Level Path
- **R** Ramp
- **S** Steps
- **G** Gate/Chicane
- **sT** Stile

Lancaster Canal Regeneration Partnership

Lancaster Canal Regeneration Partnership is a consortium of local authorities, Canal & River Trust, Inland Waterways Association, Lancaster Canal Trust and other voluntary groups. Its long-term aim is the reopening of the canal into the heart of Kendal. In the shorter tem it is engaged in projects that promote the canal as a public amenity and provide multi-user access. For more information there is a link at **www.lctrust.co.uk**

Where modern meets traditional and relaxation is the key

Crooklands Hotel, Crooklands,
Nr. Milnthorpe, Cumbria LA7 7NW
T: 015395 67432
F: 015395 67525
info@crooklands.com
www.crooklands.com

Crooklands Hotel is a family run hotel offering the personal touch, so sit back and relax with your friends and family and enjoy our hospitality. Sample local hand-pulied ales in front of our roaring open fire in our cosy bar area. Dine in either one of our two restaurants each offer a different dining experience. Old world charm of the Cottage Restaurant and a modern contemporary feel in the Jules Restaurant. Try exciting new dishes inspired from around the world, or our heady home cooked local delicacies. Why not try our famous Sunday Carvery. Crookiands Hotel has 30 well appointed en-suite bedrooms, conference facilities and can cater for private parties of up to 120 guests.

CROOKLANDS • 154 – 168

North of Holme, the canal is again culverted under the M6. Follow the signposted short diversion across the field alongside the motorway to rejoin the canal at Dukes Bridge (155). The canal and everything around is dominated by the 870 foot (265m) high Farleton Fell, which makes an impressive backdrop to this very pleasant stretch of canal. At Farleton there are the remains of a canalside packet house which was once a busy stable and a stopping point for the fast passenger packet boats, including 'Swiftsure', 'Waterwitch', 'Swallow' and 'Crewdson'. The canal is again navigable for well over a mile going past Dovehouses Bridge (161) to Moss Side Culvert (162), where the A65 crosses on an embankment, following its realignment when the M6 was built. Walkers can use the pedestrian underpass to continue along the canal for a short distance, until it is again culverted under the M6 embankment at Bridge 163a. Take the short detour onto the adjacent A65 and back onto the canal north of the motorway. The M6 leaves the canal at last and there is a further 2 mile section of canal as far as Stainton, a very attractive stretch to enjoy with a small trailable craft. Here, between Bridges 163a and 164, is the Millness slipway, available for use by licensed craft. Canal & River Trust require 24 hours notice of intended use; contact them (see p.92) for instructions on access and operation. The slipway was built for the 2006 IWA National Trailboat Festival, when some 30 visiting boats brought this section of the canal back to life for 3 days over the Easter weekend. It was refurbished for their return in 2015

The main water supply enters just south of Crooklands Aqueduct; up to 17 million gallons of water a day feed into the canal here from Killington Reservoir, 6 miles to the north east. The reservoir was completed in 1819 and holds 766 million gallons when full. Motorists get a good view of the reservoir as they stop at Killington Lake Services on the southbound carriageway of the M6 in Cumbria. At Crooklands, the offside wharf is a coal yard, once supplied via the canal. On the towpath the once-derelict stables, now completely restored by the Lancaster Canal Trust, houses a small exhibition featuring the Northern Reaches. The Trust's trip boat NB Waterwitch operates from this site, adjacent Bridge 166, on Sundays and Bank Holidays from May to September and on Saturdays in August. There is a picnic site and an explanatory panel about the role of the adjacent Wakefield's Wharf, built to serve the nearby gunpowder factory at Gatebeck.

CROOKLANDS
Bridges 154 – 168

BOATS

NB Waterwitch, Br.166. Opposite
Crooklands Hotel, LA7 7NW. Trip
boat run by the Lancaster Canal
Trust, Sundays and Bank Holidays
from May to September, plus
Saturdays in August, 11am to
4pm. Tel: 07504 710351

FOOD

Hideaway Coffe House, on A65
100yd E of Br.163a. Open daily.
Tel: 015395 67434.

PUBS

Crooklands Hotel, Bar &
Restaurant50yd E of Br.166.
Tel. 01539 567432

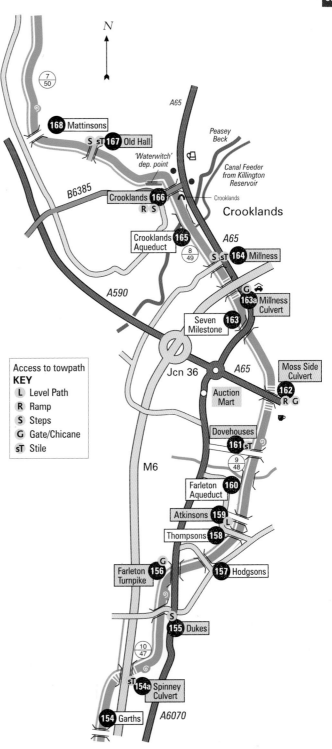

SEDGWICK • 169 – 182

The remaining section of canal provides good fishing, with tench being available. Bridge 170 is another one once equipped with stop gates, this time two pairs – covering stoppage in either direction (see also Br.146). A small feeder supplies the canal with water taken from Stainton Beck at a weir ¼ mile to the north: the Beck then shares the passage under the canal aqueduct with a public footpath. At Stainton Crossing Bridge (172) the canal is finally blocked and from here northwards is drained and partly infilled. Just before Hincaster Tunnel, the canal is split by the A590. Take the short detour along Well Heads Lane through the underpass and turn right through the gate onto a short length of towpath leading towards the tunnel portal. Follow the Horse Path over the hill to rejoin the canal at the other end of Hincaster Tunnel. The canal runs north for ¼ mile, overlooking the woods of Levens Park and the Kent valley, before it is again cut, and this time disastrously so, by the A590, which passes through a wide sloping cutting well below canal level. Leave the towpath and follow the lane on the left for ½ mile, until it crosses a bridge over the A590. At the north end of the bridge follow the finger post up the bank for a stile with a footpath sign to Hawes Bridge via towpath. Once over the stile, climb the

steep bank and look NNE for the canal bridge (177) in the distance across the field. This used to be a very impressive stretch of canal, cut into the hillside with excellent views. The canal itself was obliterated in 1985 when it was landscaped into the adjacent fields; fortunately the views remain. The line of the canal reappears at the bridge and remains as far as the grand structure of Sedgwick Aqueduct, a Scheduled Ancient Monument, which towers above the village. 200yd further on the canal is again obliterated across farmland but can be followed along the line of a hedge on the left for ¼ mile to a kissing gate in the far left hand corner of the field. It then continues for another ¼ mile through a bridge which now stands isolated in the middle of the next field and serves no purpose except as a shelter for the cattle. There are many gates and stiles on the path all the way to Kendal.

The canal bed reappears and there is a pleasant leafy walk through a cutting to Larkrigg Hall Bridge (180), where the canal comes into the open. Beyond Crow Park Bridge (181), the canal has been filled in to the level of the adjacent farmland and will not be seen again for the rest of the way to Kendal, which is now visible in the distance.

Stainton Aqueduct On Saturday 5th December 2016 the unprecedented rain storm 'Desmond' resulted in an apparent wall of water coming down Stainton Beck scouring away the foundations of the downstream abutments resulting in them becoming detached from the main structure and causing part of the towpath embankment to slip away. CR&T were concerned that the aqueduct itself could collapse or the embankment slip further, resulting in the water in this section of the canal to drain away. A temporary emergency dam was erected and the remaining section over the aqueduct to Stainton Bridge was pumped out and discharged into the newly excavated First

SEDGWICK **Bridges 169 – 182**

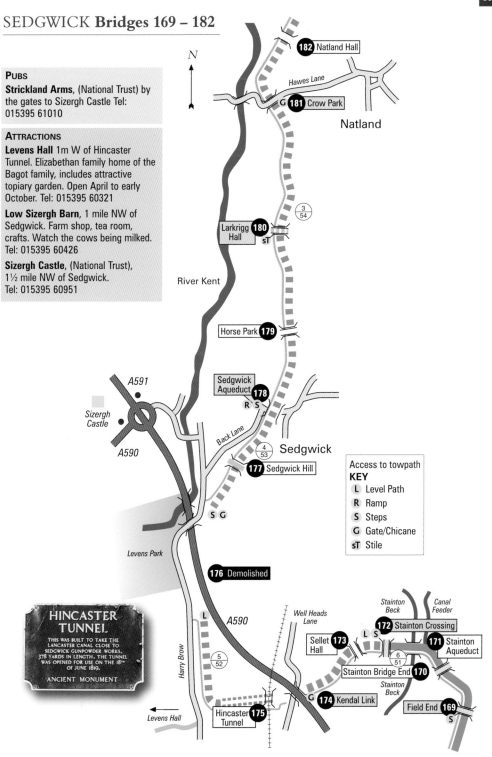

PUBS

Strickland Arms, (National Trust) by the gates to Sizergh Castle Tel: 015395 61010

ATTRACTIONS

Levens Hall 1m W of Hincaster Tunnel. Elizabethan family home of the Bagot family, includes attractive topiary garden. Open April to early October. Tel: 015395 60321

Low Sizergh Barn, 1 mile NW of Sedgwick. Farm shop, tea room, crafts. Watch the cows being milked. Tel: 015395 60426

Sizergh Castle, (National Trust), 1½ mile NW of Sedgwick. Tel: 015395 60951

Natland

River Kent

Sedgwick

A591

Sizergh Castle

A590

Back Lane

Levens Park

182 Natland Hall

Hawes Lane

G **181** Crow Park

3/54

Larkrigg Hall **180** sT

Horse Park **179**

Sedgwick Aqueduct **178** R S

4/53

177 Sedgwick Hill

S G

Access to towpath
KEY
L Level Path
R Ramp
S Steps
G Gate/Chicane
sT Stile

176 Demolished

HINCASTER TUNNEL
THIS WAS BUILT TO TAKE THE LANCASTER CANAL CLOSE TO SEDGWICK GUNPOWDER WORKS, 378 YARDS IN LENGTH. THE TUNNEL WAS OPENED FOR USE ON THE 18TH OF JUNE 1819.
ANCIENT MONUMENT

L A590

Harry Brow

5/52

Levens Hall

Hincaster **175** Tunnel

Well Heads Lane

G **174** Kendal Link

Stainton Beck   Canal Feeder

L S **172** Stainton Crossing

Sellet Hall **173**

6/51

Stainton Bridge End **170**

171 Stainton Aqueduct

Stainton Beck

Field End **169** S

Furlong channel. A more permanent clay dam has now been installed across the canal and CR&T are currently raising funds (estimated at £2m) to carry out repairs to the structure.

First Furlong The length from Br172 to Wellheads Lane (before the demolished B174) is being restored by the Lancaster Canal Trust with the generous support of the owner. The first length to Br173 the 'First Furlong' has been excavated and is currently being re-watered after which the next 400m or so will be tackled.

Hincaster Tunnel: This is 380 yards long and is the only tunnel on the canal. It was built to take barges close to Sedgwick Gunpowder Works. The tunnel has no towpath so the barges were hauled through by means of a rope fixed on a side wall, or were 'legged' through by the boatmen, by pushing against the tunnel sides with their feet. The horses were led over the tunnel along the horse path which today's walker must follow. This footpath is an interesting feature which has the status of a Scheduled Ancient Monument. The tunnel portals are listed structures. The building at the western portal is a typical stable for the swift packet boat service from Kendal to Preston. Reaching speeds of up to 12 mph between stops, the horses were changed every four or five miles; the next stables southbound can

be seen adjacent to Dukes Bridge (155) at Farleton.

Sedgwick: A small village dominated by the canal embankment and the aqueduct over the road.

Levens Hall and Park: Situated less than a mile due west of Hincaster Tunnel via the footpath to Levens Bridge. Enter the park from the road north of Hincaster Tunnel, just before it crosses the A590, and follow the famous avenue of trees south-west to the Hall. Levens Hall is the home of the Bagot family, an Elizabethan residence which was originally a medieval Pele tower and fortification against marauding border raiders. The Hall and Gardens are open to the public from April to early October, Sundays to Thursdays. Walkers using the Park are able to visit the tea-room, gift shop and plant sales area without the need to pay for admission to the Hall and Gardens. Tel: 015395 60321

Sizergh Castle: National Trust property, one mile northwest of Sedgwick between the A590 & A591, home of the Strickland family for 700 years. Impressive 14th century Pele tower, extended in Tudor times with some of the finest Elizabethan overmantels in the country. Good English and French furniture, art and Stuart relics and surrounded by beautiful gardens. Tea room. Open April to October. Tel: 015395 60951.

KENDAL • 183 – Canal Head

Kendal is a charming old stone market town on the River Kent. There are narrow cobbled streets and yards and a mediaeval Shambles. Several attractive 18th century stone bridges span the River Kent. The Gothic Parish Church, which stands alongside the river, is one of the widest in the country. Kendal is also the 'gateway' to the Lake District. The buildings and history of the industry in Kendal are well described in Kendal's Canal: History, Industry and People by John Satchell, (see p.85) Although many of the buildings associated with the early years of the canal in Kendal have been destroyed or dramatically altered, there remain many clues to the importance of the canal in the development and prosperity of Kendal after it was opened in 1819. Just north of Parkside Road there are some buildings of the Kendal Gas Light and Coke Company that opened in 1825 with coal delivered by canal to its own wharf. The original canal head basin has been infilled but some coping stones are visible just inside the council depot yard. Canal Head North and Canal Head South define the area of the original basin, and Canal Head Cottage remains as the (extended) house of the Canal Agent.

The centre of Kendal is reached by turning left at the terminus and heading west across the River Kent. Buses run from here back to Tewitfield and Carnforth and northwards into the Lake District.

From Natland to Kendal the canal has been filled in but the original line can still be followed even though it is now used as factory yards, car parks or gardens. The line of the towing path is a public right of way all the way to the terminus in Kendal. From Natland Hall Bridge, the canal ran northwards across farmland along the line of a hedge on the left, before crossing Natland Road. It ran alongside the road for a short distance to Natland Mill Bridge, where the line is again evident in a cutting.

At Kendal Changeline Bridge, the towpath changed to the east side of the canal. This is the only occurrence of a turnover bridge in Cumbria and it is a listed building. The bridge was restored in 2002 under a Kendal Civic Society initiative. The towpath is now used as a cycleway and footpath all the way to the terminus, which now houses the council depot and the public recycling collection point.

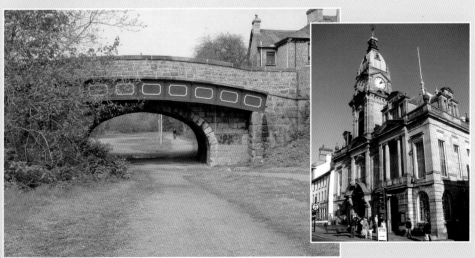

KENDAL **Bridge 183 – Canal Head**

PUBS

There are many pubs, restaurants and shops in the centre of Kendal.

ATTRACTIONS

Kendal Castle, ¼ mile E of Br.187 or Canal Head: The climb up to the Castle is well worth the effort; although much of the original Norman castle has been lost, considerable restoration has been carried out in recent years to preserve what remains. Katherine Parr, the last wife of Henry VIII, lived here with her father who was Lord of the castle.

Museum of Lakeland Life, Kirkland: Reconstructed workshops and intimate farmhouse rooms housing local industries and culture. Arts and Craft Movement display. Craft demonstrations. Admission charge. Open Mon – Sat. Tel: 01539 722464.

Abbot Hall Art Gallery, Kirkland: One of Britain's finest small, independent galleries housed in a Georgian house built in 1759, with masterpieces by George Romney, portraits by Daniel Gardner, and watercolours by John Ruskin. Coffee shop. Admission charge. Open Mon – Sat. Tel: 01539 722464.

Kendal Museum, Station Road: An indoor nature trail of realistic habitats, reconstructed to show the wealth of Lakeland natural history. It also tells the fascinating story of local people from the Stone Age to the present day. Admission charge (children free) Open Tuesday to Saturday, 10.30am to 4pm. Tel: 01539 815597.

Brewery Arts Centre, Highgate: Theatre, music, films, exhibitions. Café, resturant and bar. Tel 01539 722833

Quaker Tapestry, Stramongate: 77 unique panels chronicling Quaker life throughout the centuries. Admission charge. Open Mon – Sat, café. Tel 01539 722975.

K Village, The Lakes Outlet Mall, Lound Road Tel: 01539 732363

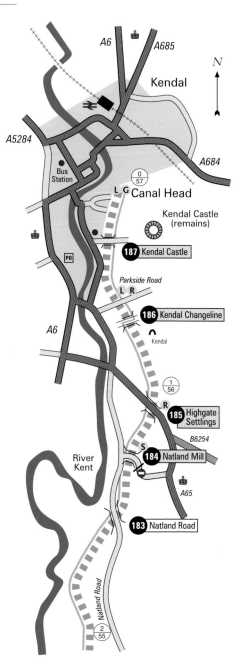

INFORMATION ON THE LANCASTER CANAL

Public Transport

The position of the canal on its north/south axis makes it an ideal base for exploring much of North Lancashire and South Cumbria. The canal is well served by both rail and bus services.

Trains

The west coast main line from London to Glasgow runs parallel to the canal. There are major stations at Preston, Lancaster and Oxenholme. From Preston, trains are available to Blackpool and the Fylde coast, Blackburn, Clitheroe, Burnley, Leeds, Manchester and Liverpool. Lancaster is the junction for services to Morecambe and Carnforth. From Carnforth the branch line continues to Barrow-in-Furness, through Silverdale, Arnside and Grange-over-Sands, and is well worth a trip for the picturesque countryside and coast of Furness and South Lakeland. This line continues along the west coast of Cumbria, providing access to the Ravenglass & Eskdale Railway, Sellafield,, the towns of West Cumbria and finally Carlisle. Lancaster and Carnforth also serve the line to Skipton and Leeds, with access to the Settle to Carlisle line. Oxenholme junction is the start of the branch to Kendal and Windermere. More details at www.nationalrail.co.uk Tel: 03457 484950.

Buses

The main operator in the area is Stagecoach Cumbria and North Lancashire. Other services are operated by the municipal undertakings in the main towns and of course Blackpool has its famous trams which operate along the coast to Fleetwood. Blackpool is accessible by bus from Preston, Garstang and Lancaster. A service operates from Lancaster up the Lune valley to Kirkby Lonsdale and to Ingleton, famous for its waterfalls. An hourly service operates from Preston direct to the Trafford Centre in Manchester. In South Cumbria the main route serving the canal is the 555 service from Lancaster to Kendal, via Carnforth, Burton in Kendal, Holme and Milnthorpe. From Kendal there are services to Windermere and Keswick and to Sedbergh in the Yorkshire Dales.

Buses are particularly useful for access on and off the canal as the principal routes between towns in this area cross the canal at numerous points. Bus stops close to canal bridges are marked on the strip maps and the principal routes are listed below.

Bus No.	Between Towns	at Canal Bridge Nos
35	Preston bus station and Tanterton	10
80	Preston, Myerscough	10, 12, 32(80), 35(82)
68,	Preston, Kirkham, Blackpool	10–12
61	Preston, Lytham, St Annes, Blackpool	10, 12, MRLink, Br.A
42	Lancaster, Garstang, Poulton-le-Fylde, Blackpool	59, 62, 81, 86, 99, 102
40, 41	Morecambe, Lancaster, Garstang, Preston	42, 44, 45, 47, 49, 59, 62, 81, 86, 99, 102
5	Morecambe, Carnforth	118–128
80,	Lancaster, Ingleton	102, 106
81	Lancaster, Kirkby Lonsdale	108
55	Lancaster, Carnforth	110, 121–128
555	Lancaster, Carnforth, Kendal, Windermere, Ambleside, Grasmere, Keswick	102, 110, 121–128, 139, 149, 177, 187
X6	Kendal, Grange, Ulverston, Barrow in Furness	187, Canal Head
567	Kendal, Kirkby Lonsdale	166, 187, Canal Head

This information is correct at the time of publication but may change.

More details from Traveline, 0871 200 22 33, www.traveline.info or Tourist Information Centres.

INFORMATION ON THE LANCASTER CANAL

Boats

Lancaster Canal Trust offers short cruises from Crooklands Bridge (166) on nb Waterwitch on a 2 mile isolated section of the canal. Generally operating on Sundays and bank holidays from May to September & Saturdays in August, 11am to 4pm. The boat is also available for charter trips for schools, clubs and private parties. Tel: 07504 710351 or visit www.lctrust.co.uk for details.

Lancaster Canal Boats operates a waterbus service between Barton Grange Marina and Tewitfield between March and October. Speciality Lune Aqueduct cruises, award winning special evening cruises and private group & party hire of the luxury 'Kingfisher' vessel are also available. Tel: 01524 389410 or visit www.budgietransport.co.uk for details.

Cycle Hire

Sunshine Cycles, Morecambe. (4 miles NW of Lancaster by bus). Tel: 01524 414709

Leisure Lakes Bikes, Penny Street, Lancaster, 200yds S, Br99, Tel: 01524 844389

Access for All

See notes on page 19 about towpath access for wheelchairs and buggies and for those with limited mobility.

BOAT HIRE, MARINAS & SERVICES ON THE LANCASTER CANAL

See adverts or the coloured panel on the appropriate Map page for details.

Arlen Hire Boats, Br.10 – Marina services.
Blackleach Marina, Br.31 – Mooring only.
Pendle Marine Br.32 – Marina services.
Moons Bridge Marina, Br.36 – Marina services.
Lancaster Canal Cruises, Br.44-45 – Charter trip boat hire.
Barton Grange Marina, Br.47 – Marina services.
Lancaster Canal Boats, Br.47 – Waterbus, special cruises and charters.
Water Farm Boat Hire, Br.47 – Narrowboat hire.
Crabtree Narrowboat Hire, Br 47 – Narrowboat hire.
'The Margaret Kane', Br 47 – Wheelchair accessible hotel boat.
Bridge House Marina Br.64-65 – Marina services, Dayboat hire.
Garstang Marina, Br.65-66 – Marina services.
Water Babies Narrowboat Hire, Br 78 – Narrowboat hire.
BWML Glasson Basin Marina – Marina services.
BWML Galgate Marina, Br.86. – Mooring, sanitary station, water.
Lancaster Canal Boats, Br 99 – Waterbus, special cruises and charters.
Nu-Way Acorn Marina, Br.127-128 – Marina services.
Tewitfield Marina, Br.138-139 – Mooring only.
Bluebell Narrowboat Holidays, Tewitfield Marina
Duck Island Boat Company, Tewitfield Marina
Blossom Time, Tewitfield Marina

Sanitary stations and water points at Cadley, Bilsborrow, Garstang, Galgate, Lancaster, Carnforth and Tewitfield. Additional water points at or near bridges 32 & 86

MAPS OF THE LANCASTER CANAL

OS Landranger (1:50,000);	102 – Preston & Blackpool	97 – Kendal & Morecambe
OS Explorer series (1:25,000);	286 – Blackpool & Preston	OL41 – Forest of Bowland & Ribblesdale,
	296 – Lancaster, Morecambe & Fleetwood	OL7 – The English Lakes, SE Area.

GEOprojects publish a useful and informative map of Lancaster Canal & Ribble Link

INFORMATION ON THE LANCASTER CANAL

BOOKS ON THE LANCASTER CANAL
The following books are out of print but second-hand copies can be obtained

Building the Lancaster Canal: Robert Philpotts. Blackwater Books. ISBN 978-0-946623-00-6

The Lancaster Canal in Focus: Janet Rigby. Landy Publishing. ISBN 978-1-872895-72-7

Life on the Lancaster Canal: Janet Rigby. Landy Publishing. ISBN 978-1-872895-66-6

Lancaster Canal Walks: Mary Welsh. Cicerone Press. ISBN 978-1-85284-138-6

55 '555' Walks: Robert Swain. Yan Press ISBN 978-0-9540713-0-1

A Walker's Guide to the Lancaster Canal: Robert Swain, Cicerone Press. ISBN 978-1-85284-055-6

Canals of North West England: C Hadfield & G Biddle. David & Charles. ISBN 978-0-7153-4956-4

Kendal's Canal: John Satchell. Kendal Civic Society. ISBN 978-0-9509869-1-3

TOURIST INFORMATION CENTRES

Preston	Town Hall, Lancaster Road. PR1 2RL	Tel: 01772 253731
Lytham St Annes	Town Hall, St Annes Road West. FY8 1LW	Tel: 01253 658443
Blackpool	Festival House, Promenade FY1 1AP	Tel: 01253 478222
Fleetwood	Marine Hall, Esplanade FY7 6HF	Tel: 01253 887693
Garstang	Unit 1, Cherestanc Sq. PR3 1EF (by Booths)	Tel: 01995 602125
Morecambe	Old Station Bldgs, Marine Rd Central. LA4 4DB	Tel: 01524 582808
Lancaster	The Storey, Meeting House Lane. LA1 1TH	Tel: 01524 582394
Kendal	Made in Cumbria, 48a Branthwaite Brow LA9 4TX	Tel: 01539 735891

These offices can supply leaflets and up to date opening times for all places of interest mentioned in this guide – plus information on transport, walks and specialist activities.

See also www.visitlancashire.com and www.visitcumbria.com

For local arts, crafts, food & drink etc. see www.madeinlancs.co.uk and www.madeincumbria.co.uk

Arnside & Silverdale AONB Unit, Tel: 01524 761034 www.arnsidesilverdaleaonb.org.uk

EMERGENCIES ON THE LANCASTER CANAL

Accidents or incidents on the canal: Canal & River Trust, Freephone Canals; Tel: **0800 47 999 47**

Personal illness or injury: If it is obviously an ambulance case then phone **999** and give the nearest road bridge number, the road name and the nearest village or town.

In less urgent cases phone **111**

Royal Lancaster Infirmary A&E is 100yd S of Br.99

Vets for Pets – *a selection chosen only for their proximity to the canal:*

Riverbank Veterinary Centre, Watery Lane, Preston, PR2 2NN. ½ mile W of Ashton Basin. Tel: 01772 726745

Lanes Vets, Green Lane, Garstang, PR3 1PR. ½ mile N of Br.63a along A6, then R at traffic lights. Tel: 01995 603349

Burch Tree Vets, 43 Gladstone Terrace, Bulk Road, Lancaster, LA1 1DW. 100yd W of Br.103 & 104. Tel: 01524 63732

Burch Tree Vets, 39 Lancaster Road, Carnforth. LA5 9LD. 200yd N of Canal Turn pub. Tel: 01524 720002

Alison Lee, 2 Queen Street, off Lancaster Road, Carnforth, LA5 9EB. 50yd S of Canal Turn pub. Tel: 01524 735249

USEFUL ADDRESSES

For all communications relating to the Lancaster Canal contact:

Canal & River Trust Trencherfield Mill, Heritage Way. Wigan WN3 4BN Tel: **0303 040 4040** email; enquiries.northwest@canalrivertrust.org.uk

Customer Services (Milton Keynes) for general queries, licensing etc. Tel: **0303 040 4040** email; customerservices@canalrivertrust.org.uk

Inland Waterways Association Island House, Moor Road, Chesham HP5 1WA Tel: **01494 783453** www.waterways.org.uk Email the local branch at lancsandcumbria@waterways.org.uk

Lancaster Canal Boat Club, Membership Secretary Sheila Kenney **07909 646207** or **01772 452296**

Association of Cruising Enthusiasts Membership Secretary, Mrs M. Newton **01253 358453**

Lancaster Canal Trust c/o Lancaster District CVS The Cornerstone, Sulyard Street Lancaster LA1 1PX www.lctrust.co.uk